Mutilating the Body

Mutilating the Body:
Identity in Blood and Ink

Kim Hewitt

Bowling Green State University Popular Press
Bowling Green, OH 43403

Library of Congress Cataloging-in-Publication Data
Hewitt, Kim.
    Mutilating the body : identity in blood and ink / Kim Hewitt.
        p.   cm.
    Includes bibliographical references and index.
    ISBN 0-87972-709-8 (cloth). -- ISBN 0-87972-710-1 (pbk.)
    1. Self-mutilation. 2. Tattooing. 3. Body piercing. I. Title.
RC552.S4H48   1996
391'.65--dc20   96-35524
                                                                                    CIP

Cover design by Laura Darnell-Dumm

Contents

Preface
A Memory of Blood and Ink

What lies deepest of all in man is the skin.
—Paul Valery

My memories are fuzzy—I don't remember chronological sequence or how old I was. I think it started when I was about 13. I remember being out on the soccer field one day in gym class and looking at the cuts on my arm. Funny, in my memory it's a sunny day and I don't remember feeling any emotional anything really. Just wondering what people would say if they saw my cuts and then hoping they wouldn't ever see them. I think I was a sophomore at the time, but that wasn't the first cutting time. I remember once, maybe the very first time, being alone in someone's apartment. I searched the bathroom cabinet for razor blades, found some and made some tiny, tiny nicks on my wrist. Now that I write I think maybe this happened much much later, maybe while my father was in the hospital dying of cancer—one of the last times I cut myself as a teenager. As I nicked my wrist I said to myself, "This is a promise that someday I will love someone." Maybe what I really wanted was reassurance that someday someone would love me.

When I was 14 I had times of darkness. I remember kneeling by my bed with my hands over my face. I felt deaf, dumb, blind. I couldn't move for what seemed a very long time. Sometimes it was daytime and sometimes it was nighttime. I don't know if this happened right before cutting spells, but I know they are somehow related. In bad times still the physical memory of crouching on the floor, hot, sweating, paralyzed, returns.

When I cut the first time I was crazy with fury. My mother was angry with my father—so angry—so incredibly angry—and it was eating me up. I couldn't talk to her, couldn't tell her to shut up. I went to my room and saw a metal can tab on my table. I began scraping my skin, just scrapes, just pink, just raw, just bleeding a little. These marks made the multiple thin scars on my forearm. I kept that tab in a special place on my desk. It was there when I needed it. I didn't always use it, didn't even think about it that much. Then the blind anger would come and I would attack my skin—the inside of my upper arm where no one would see the marks. Even I didn't have to look at the ugly wounds. I'd dig into the flesh until the blood began to flow. I don't remember ever feeling pain during the cutting, although eventually I'd get queasy at the sight of the blood. I'd feel satisfied too though, and I never washed off the blood. I remember lying in bed and feeling it smart and it felt good. Always the same spot, opening the old wound. This created the wide white scars on the inside of my upper arm. Sometimes my mother would notice the scars, but I always evaded her questions and she would go on to something else.

When I was 21 I cut myself after an argument with my partner. He sobbed as he washed the blood off my arm and kept asking me why I had done it. I couldn't tell him. The shame of that night followed me for days and the pain and sorrow it caused both of us never left. It seems like years that I walked around with my arms glued to my sides so people wouldn't see, and even now I am self-conscious about my scars. I see people look at them, sometimes lovers ask what they are and I almost never tell them. They almost never know. If they do, they don't let on. When I see scars on other people's skin, I notice. I wonder who or what made them.

My scars have flattened over the years. My body is eating the scar tissue away. Several years ago a close friend confessed that she had been cutting herself. As I listened to her I realized for the first time that I wasn't alone. I realized the body has a private landscape without words, and I knew I had to find a language to talk about my scars.

Acknowledgments

I would like to thank Robert Abzug, Ricardo Ainslie, and Linda Montano at the University of Texas in Austin for supporting and believing in this project. It is also a pleasure to thank Joel Dinerstein and Ina Szekely for their warmth and intellectual companionship, as well as John Davis for the time he so graciously diverted from his own projects to support me in every way possible and to provide photographs. Thanks to the people whose decisions to express their identity and spirituality upon their bodies inspired me and who so generously shared their stories with me. Many thanks to all the people who encouraged me.

Introduction

Why do people inflict pain upon themselves, especially when the process results in a permanent mark upon the body? This is a profound question. In seeking an answer, I focused initially on tattoos, and my research began by asking individuals about their chosen marks. Although some of the answers I received were well thought out and showed remarkable insight and self-awareness, many were unsatisfactory. Some replied that they "just wanted a tattoo" or "just liked the design." My desire to probe deeper was prompted by an adamant belief that actions speak louder than words, and that often individuals are unwilling or unable to fully articulate the complex motivations for their actions. Research about the history of tattooing customs illuminated their universality, their social and spiritual significance in many cultures, and their similarity to other procedures that break skin and draw blood as part of culturally sanctioned rituals. I began to see tattooing as one form of a much broader kind of secular and spiritual writing upon the body in which the body is used as primary material for self-expression. I decided to focus on forms of body modification that Western cultures have often defined as pathologically unhealthy, stigmatized as deviant, or imposed upon marginalized members of society. For the purposes of this book I am not including the various daily acts of self-mutilation such as tweezing, hair-cutting, or plastic surgery. Although these acts recreate the human body and function to socialize the individual, they lost any aura of stigma long ago and are so common as to go noticed.[1]

At a glance the acts of self-mutilation discussed in this text may seem unrelated. At first, they may not even appear to be acts of self-mutilation. Some people may object to my use of the term *mutilation*, especially when discussing practices that adorn the body. According to *Webster's New International Dictionary of the English Language*, *mutilate* means to "cut off or remove a limb or essential part of; to maim; cripple; hack, to destroy or remove a material part of so as to render imperfect," while *adorn* means "to

1

embellish; render pleasing or attractive, add to the beauty, splendor or attractiveness of." Although these definitions at first seem contradictory, I believe only the troublesome phrase "to render imperfect" presents a problem. Perfection is an intangible concept held in the imagination, and to equate wholeness with perfection shows a cultural bias that is difficult to insist upon with any consistency, either globally or even within Western culture. Simple actions such as hair tweezing and nail clipping are subtractive but are performed to achieve greater beauty and perfection in the eye of the beholder. Many parents circumcise their male children for aesthetic and cultural reasons and do not consider this an act of mutilation. Tattooing and piercing, while embellishing the human body, usually remove and replace flesh and blood. To say that these actions mutilate or maim the body is not a judgment upon their ability to adorn the body, or render it either more perfect or imperfect. My goal is not to pass judgment upon people who choose to adorn their bodies with tattoos or piercings, or individuals with eating disorders, or individuals who cut or otherwise alter their bodies. My purpose here is to place these actions within a conceptual framework that explores their similarities and dissimilarities. Placing these actions relative to each other creates a new context in which to understand their meaning for individuals and for the culture in which they occur. I ultimately interpret them as acts that ask to be witnessed—acts not only of self-expression but self-initiation and sometimes self-medication. Perhaps the most accurate term would be self-evolution. I will explore these acts as positive expressions of social custom, individualism, and resourcefulness. I believe they are often symptomatic of crises in identity, religious faith, and modern social structure, and are acts that help resolve those crises.

The acts of body modification I discuss also spring from a deep, universal motive. Although many of the actions analyzed here are ancient tools performed in a modern context very different from the cultural setting in which they were originally performed, the underlying function of providing humanity with an avenue of symbolic death and rebirth remains the same. While non-Western small-village cultures may perform these acts of self-mutilation as parts of rituals in which many members of society participate, in Western society the individual must search for witnesses, and often relies on a larger, less familiar, often less willing, public audience. In Hegel's model of the interdependence of the master and slave, the master requires the slave as a witness to affirm selfhood and power, as the slave likewise requires a master to affirm self-worth. When one member of the partnership is missing, an individual must strive to fulfill both roles and must become actor and spectator, exhibitionist and witness, punisher and punished, master and slave, victor and victim. Expressed in developmental terms, the individual is both parent and child, authority and rebel, in the effort to become whole, mature, and autonomous. The individual seeks to transform and parent him or her self. Similar to a religious conversion experience, self-mutilators confess their "sins" and testify, sometimes to a public audience, sometimes only to themselves. Body mutilation has the power to purify and recreate, and push an individual further along the path of self-evolution.

The parallel between transformation of the body and religious conversion is an important one. While acts of contemporary self-mutilation in Western society may be related to the lack of a unifying religion embraced by the whole culture, I prefer to explore them not as replacements for religion but as actions that attempt to fulfill spiritual needs similar to those fulfilled by organized religions. Likewise, these acts of self-alteration may create private and cultural spaces that fulfill a need for community and cultural inclusion. In a religious milieu, the act of confessing requires witness of the confessor both as an individual and as a member of a social structure that will continue to support his or her new identity. An important question is whether or not acts of self-mutilation accomplish successful self-transformation. The answer is contingent upon social reception and support of the action as an avenue of rebirth.

The attempts at self-transformation discussed in this text, and the discussion of them as interrelated pieces of a larger whole, is important for several reasons. That acts previously considered pathological and deviant are now considered part of a mainstream cultural discourse illuminates a renewed interest in the human body as territory for establishing personal, social, and spiritual identity. In turn, discussing the uses of the human body in overlapping spheres of private, social, and cosmic meaning, confirms the significance of popular culture and individual actions as both creating and reflecting cultural meaning. The human body is the oldest and most persistent vehicle for humanity's creative impulses, and interest in tattooing and piercing continues to increase as the public becomes more aware of the potency of body art. Images and discussion of body art are filtering into mainstream discourse and are redefining our ideas of beauty and physical perfection.

Psychological and cultural theories aid exploration of actions that are painful, chosen, and leave marks upon the body. Chapters 1 and 2 will address beliefs that entwine the body with spirituality and the pertinence of initiation rituals that circumscribe the body as both spiritual and social territory. Shifting focus from cultural dynamics to individual manipulation of the body, I will present Heinz Kohut's theory of the narcissistic self to explain the theory of modern body narcissism and the use of pain to reintegrate a fragmented self. These chapters explicate the theory that body modification is an attempt to establish an identity within a cultural milieu that includes both the immediate family environment and a broader social sphere. If cultural rituals meant to define coming of age spiritually or socially do not exist, individuals may create private rituals to fulfill similar functions. Some individuals may create public rituals to commemorate their passage from one state to another and gain recognition of their transformation.

Chapter 3 will analyze eating disorders as masochistic attempts to establish autonomy and ritualistic attempts to transform the self. Understanding the significance of fasting as a religious activity contributes to an understanding of eating disorders as quasi-religious activity. Individuals with eating disorders often self-mutilate as an attempt to reintegrate themselves with their surrounding social milieu, and this section will explore self-mutilation as an effort to combat a state of psychological disassociation. Ritual theory provides culturally accepted models with which to understand the roles of fasting and self-mutilation in the process of differentiation and social inclusion. This section will also delineate the reasons why prisoners and other institutionalized populations self-mutilate. This section will demonstrate the importance of cultural witnessing and interpretation. Actions considered deviant in one milieu may be viewed as wholly appropriate in another.

Recent ethnographic literature reveals that many individuals who tattoo, pierce, and scar their bodies are seeking to express their individuality and affiliation with subcultural groups. Others seek to manifest a spirituality that embraces the body rather than opposes it, and I will synthesize this information with the psychological theories explaining body narcissism and "deviant" self-mutilation. The cultural and historical significance of fasting, tattooing, and scarification imbues body modification with the power to demolish Greco-Christian prohibitions on the "imperfect" body, and the power to re-establish the body and its sensations of pain and pleasure, as integral elements of spirituality and social identity. In chapter 4 I acknowledge the secularization of spirituality as it implodes upon the body, and the convergence of cosmic and social meanings. I will discuss the way in which painful acts of self-adornment confirm social status, and establish or embellish individual identity in mainstream and subcultural society.

Chapter 5 will discuss ways in which artists and youth subcultures self-mutilate for conscious display in the public sphere. Although many artists of the 1960s and 1970s provoked the viewing public to reconsider the human body as a medium for expression, I limit my discussion to several performance artists who chose to render painful acts of self-mutilation. The street performance aesthetic of the punk movement is seminal to the secularization and popularization of self-mutilation. The self-harming and self-degrading behavior of the punk subculture reveals a message of rebellion and affinity with marginalized groups that has influenced the continued popularity of body art.

Because of the nature of deviance as a culturally relative concept, I use a pragmatic definition. Temporarily ignoring pathological lack of remorse, I will consider as "deviant" or "perverse" behavior that the individual feels is morally wrong, but which he or she cannot adapt to quell the accompanying feelings of shame provoked by the behavior. As Louise Kaplan notes, the key ingredients of perversity are "desperation and fixity."[2] This definition cannot be excised from social context, and I fully acknowledge that even this definition rests on cultural constructs of what is and is not shameful. This definition allows me to consider the behaviors often labeled as deviant as part of a continuum. Behaviors that range from individually dysfunctional to culturally noteworthy may exhibit similar intrapsychic foundations. This is the basis for synthesizing what I believe to be a continuum of self-mutilatory behaviors ranging from self-starvation to performance art in which the performer draws her own blood, to the trendy fashion of navel piercing. According to my chosen definition of *deviant*, these actions would be aberrant only when they become so compelling as to be immutable. Acts of "fixity and desperation" lose the integrity of choice.

6 Mutilating the Body

Acts of painful adornment establish a continuum between self-stigmatizing with self-inflicted pain and fashionable social behaviors. Public and private self-mutilation of the body are redefining aesthetics, marginality, and spirituality according to the parameters of symbolic and real pain. Although acts of self-mutilation may indicate pathology, they may also be attempts to self-heal, or at least self-medicate. More benign forms of self-mutilation, which are ornamental and artistic, albeit also painful, may also be attempts at healing individual and social disintegration. By analyzing the roots of the body modification trend I will locate a common thread between the forms of self-mutilation discussed and emphasize that the desire of individuals to acquire marks of self-stigmatization expresses a change in how society perceives marginalization. Painful body modification is an expression of an American preoccupation with coming of age, individuation, and marginalization. By using pain and by changing the body, individuals are attempting to recreate themselves and write the story of their identity upon their bodies.

1

Etching Identity on the Body

The body is to be compared, not to a physical object, but rather to a work of art . . . it is a focal point of living meanings, not the function of a certain number of mutually variable terms.
—Maurice Merleau-Ponty[1]

The Magical Body

Marking the human body may be not only the most ancient art form but also the oldest practice of religion as a systematic expression of a belief that unseen extraordinary powers affect the course of natural and human events, and that humans have the ability to affect these supernatural forces. Many ancient cultures inscribed the body with protective symbols and manipulated the body in rituals designed to communicate with gods and spirits. As a form of prayer, this supplication offers the human body as religious text upon which spiritual beliefs can be written and read. Eventually humankind supplemented the language of the body with spoken language, and began to substitute other behaviors for marking and modifying the human body. As the structures of societies changed, religions also changed. Written language gained prominence and in the Western world expansive systems of social hierarchy required new forms of social control. Many contemporary religions still encourage ritualistic fasting, symbolic baptism, and other uses of the body to augment religious devotion, but place more importance on organized churches, leaders, and texts to convey religious doctrine and provide an avenue for participation and redemption.

However, in many societies the body has remained the fundamental medium for expressing spiritual beliefs, and an integral part of religious practice. These practices are often disparaged as superstitious, primitive magic by adherents to modern organized religion, rationalists, and many members of the psychological community. The magical world view acknowledges the validity of alternative states of consciousness, which have been dismissed by post-Enlightenment thinkers and pathologized by modern medicine. Only recently have transpersonal anthropologists, psychologists, and ethnologists begun to investigate the pragmatic uses of magical religious practices and beliefs and their real repercussions. If we hope to understand the nature of humankind and their interaction with the cosmos it is important to step beyond the dualistic models of culture versus biology, and body versus spirit. Only then can we realize the implications of religious practices, cultural trends appropriating customs of other belief systems, and the importance of humankind's compulsion to alter the body.[2]

The belief that body alteration can mediate between earthly and spiritual levels of consciousness is based on a view of the cosmos that accepts man's ability to interact directly with spiritual forces. This belief has often been misconstrued as primitive or neurotic. In *Totem and Taboo* Sigmund Freud correctly describes ancient magical practices as manifesting an animistic "system of thought . . . that allows us to grasp the whole universe as a single unity from a single point of view," but then pathologizes this system.[3] Animists attribute spiritual existence to all people, plants, animals, and inanimate objects and recognize a web of physical and psychic connections between all of these entities. These connections allow believers to ascribe powerful magical properties to objects that resemble each other or have been in contact with a potent object or person. Although Freud is insightful in claiming that magical practices are attempts to "gain mastery over men, beasts and things,"[4] he misinterprets two essential characteristics about the animistic belief system, both of which are important to realize if we are to understand the importance of human body marking.

Freud's description of magical beliefs as narcissistic is based on his interpretation that they are beliefs in the "omnipotence of thoughts,"[5] in which humankind believes that thoughts can control and order the world. What Freud fails to see is that the animistic world view belongs to a cultural system that does not divide the individual into mind versus body, or experiences into natural versus supernatural. Animism is not based on the potency of thought but on the potency of a world in which an individual is not compartmentalized into mental, spiritual, and physical existence unable to access the simultaneous world of cosmic forces. Human beings are part of the natural world, not separate from it or the "supernatural" world that exists at the same time and place.

The contrast between this holistic world view and a Christian Anglo-European world view that separates humanity from the heavenly realm is evident in African-influenced religions in the Americas and the white Christian response to them. Although complicated by racism and the fear of slave-uprisings, Anglo-European Christians rejected the African-influenced beliefs and practices that incorporated humans and their bodies, and other everyday profane objects into the religious experience. Although they may have resorted to them on occasion, Anglo-European Christians in the New World officially denied the efficacy of charms and amulets to work hoodoo magic, and that spirits possessed and communicated with believers. The idea that the physical world could be connected to the spiritual world was considered primitive and barbaric. In the days of slavery in America, Anglo-European Christians were often appalled at the sensuousness of the religious experience of slaves and often banned sing-ing, drumming, and dancing. Within Christian sects, the Western world view dictated that the body was to be restrained in worship. In contrast, the holistic religions were compelled to integrate the body into worship practices. Members of African-influenced Christian churches often tangibly felt their religion. They sometimes fell into trances or experienced illnesses that they read as spiritual signs of their need to repent. Once saved, they felt their faith so emotionally and physically that they could not help expressing their joy with their bodies.[6] Even today, the members of many non-Anglo-European based Christian churches "get the spirit," "get happy," experience their religious ecstasy physically and express it by singing and shouting. These practices are not as extreme as the practices of African-based religions in Brazil, Cuba, or Haiti in which particular spirits possess and communicate through human bodies, but still express a holistic attitude that claims the body as spiritual territory at least for the period of religious bliss. Feeling the Holy Spirit has real tangible consequences that can be seen and heard, sung and shouted.

By excluding the holistic dimension of magical practices, Freud does not allow for real consequences, and instead calls physical responses to magical practices "motor hallucinations."[7] Accordingly, the physical response to a magical or religious practice is unimportant. Further, Freud does not address the cultural response to the frequently ritualized practice of magic. A salient example is the permanent physical change incurred during an initiation rite as the initiate is tattooed, scarred, or circumcised.

The physical changes recreate the body of the initiate and are important to the resolution and efficacy of the ceremony within the community. Not only is this ritual act of body magic important for its ability to permanently transform the psyche and world view—and thus spirituality—of the initiate, but is especially significant because it is embedded in cultural beliefs. The values of the initiate's community affirm his or her values, and vice versa. The ritual and its accompanying body marks physically socialize the initiate, who will henceforth occupy a new social status.

The second mistake Freud makes is in not acknowledging magical practices as forms of what the modern world calls art. Freud is brilliant in his assessment that art can provoke emotional effects that incur "magical" consequences. As he says, "[T]here can be no doubt that art did not begin as art for art's sake. It worked originally in the service of impulses which are for the most part extinct today. And among them we may suspect the presence of many magical purposes." Although Freud acknowledges the power of art to "produce emotional effects . . . just as though it were something real," he misses the pre-modern lack of distinction between art, religion, and magic.[8]

The "magical" art of body painting illustrates many non-Western approaches to the body as spiritual territory. Before the Greek idealization of the body and configuration of beauty as a standard Platonic essence, and before written religions circumscribed the body as the work of God to be left unmarred, man's body mediated between earthly and spiritual elements. In some belief systems this is still true. Painting the body or donning a mask or costume allows the participant to assume a different demeanor and role in preparation for communication with the spiritual world. Ritual adornment not only transforms the body but enhances the ability of the participant to enter other states of consciousness and receive divine messages. In the Baule culture of the Ivory Coast spirit mediums paint their eyes and mouths to aid clairvoyance.[9] In traditional Yoruban ancestor worship, special *Egungun* costumes and masks are employed to encourage the spirits of ancestor to materialize and converse with the family. The ritual clothing is a full body mask that contains the distilled energy of generations of family members who have carefully sewn and preserved the cloth. The person who wears the special attire channels this collective energy toward attracting the ancestor spirit, and assumes the spiritual powers of the ancestor he represents. Although the ceremonial possession of the *Egungun* costume by the ancestor is encouraged by other ritual elements of music and special foods, it is made possible by the physical act of transforming the appearance of the body.[10]

Body art affects the viewer as well as the painted or masked person. Making the body colorful, strange, and less human-looking induces in the mind of the viewer confusion that may be disturbing or delightful, or both. The person who is painted and masked in a religious ceremony is no longer recognizable as an individual, but assumes a persona of unworldly dimensions. This induces a "sacred awe"[11] in the witnessing community that allows it to communicate with supernatural realms and address dreams, anxieties, and illnesses. The masked or painted person may become possessed by a spirit or enter an altered state, at the same time cultivating an altered state in the audience. Painting, tattooing, and adorning the body may also deflect evil forces and protect the adorner by making him or her unrecognizable to hostile spirits. In the nineteenth century, for example, some Native Alaskans used tattoos and soot markings to protect themselves from the spirits of people and animals they had killed.[12] Body modification, like other art, provokes emotional and aesthetic responses in the artists and the viewers.

Specific body alterations often connote social as well as spiritual status. Masking the body with paint, tattoos, and scarification transforms it and covers it physically and psychologically but simultaneously exposes inner qualities and mystical truths. In tribal societies in which climate and custom permit scant clothing, body painting and adornment are common, and considered to be artistically and socially valuable.[13] Marking the body enculturates and differentiates an individual, and the precise meaning of body modification is unique for each person and each society. Marking the body may bestow a specific role in the community, celebrate the passage into sexual maturity, or confirm spiritual experience. According to Michel Thevoz, "In savage societies the marking was applied to the body of the 'naked ape' in order to wrench him free from nature, from animality, from meaninglessness, and to initiate him into the symbolic order."[14] In cultures that reify spiritual forces in everyday items and events, the body is considered meaningful beyond its mechanistic ability to function. It is an avenue to social and spiritual meaning, and allows humankind to write their past, present, and future upon the intimate and yet public self of their physical being.

As part of a spiritual belief system body alteration signals willingness to connect with forces existing beyond material, functional existence. Manipulating the body without opprobrium expresses a willingness to accept many layers of selfhood, truth, and development through time, as well as a belief in humankind's ability and responsibility to effect change in earthly and spiritual domains. In some forms it signals a desire to transcend not only the animal world in which extreme self-adornment is rare but also a merely human world. Self-adornment and self-recreation, while emphasizing the physicality of the body, place one in the realm of the gods. This may or may not violate cultural norms.

In many cultures respect for the body is based on a respect for order, boundaries, purity, and wholeness. According to Bakhtin, the bourgeois classical canon that evolved in Europe during the Renaissance emphasized an aesthetic of beauty based on "the conception of the complete, atomized being." The classic body is separate from other beings, symmetrical, cleansed of any connection to birth, death, or daily profane functioning. It is self-contained. It is isolated from both "the ancestral body of people" and therefore without a history, and self-sufficient, "a strictly completed, finished product," whose "inner processes of absorbing and ejecting are not revealed." These characteristics are synonymous with sanctity. In contrast, the "grotesque body" of the Middle Ages and the folk culture that transgressed the classical canon is very strongly associated with daily bodily functions, birth, and death. "It is unfinished, it outgrows itself, transgresses its own limits." It is the body in the process of becoming. It "stands on the threshold of the grave and the crib."[15] Unlike the classic body, its boundaries are open to transformation. While the classic body is free from the mortal and animal functions of living and dying, it is also unable to transcend its own stasis. The closed body with its well-established boundaries opposes the open body with its shifting boundaries and ability to metamorphose. It is often the contrast between these two concepts of the body that imbues each with symbolic force. Central to the difference is the definition of body boundaries.

The body is a vehicle for interaction between people and consequently often serves as a symbol of society. According to Mary Douglas, "Its boundaries can represent any boundaries which are threatened or precarious."[16] The body and its treatment may symbolize or directly express cultural conflicts, confusions, religious beliefs, and positive social interactions. Creating an obviously artificial appearance, for example, with body painting, masks, or tattooing, can be seen as undermining the integrity and unity of the classical body.[17] This may be an act of denial of the imperfections of the body, or an act of rebellion against cultural norms of beauty if it is performed contrary to social approval. In either case, it exemplifies a universal desire to be reborn as an object of one's own making. As part of a cultural system it is proof of an individual's acquiescence to cultural norms.

The connection between control of the body and social structure is made explicit by Mary Douglas in *Natural Symbols*, although her interpretation needs refinement. Building on the theory of Marcel Mauss who asserted the impossibility of a natural body unaffected by culture, Douglas points out that the acculturation of the body is an intimate reflection of how closely social structures control an individual's behavior. A social system that maintains stringent control over an individual will require an individual to maintain rigid control over his body. As pressure to restrict the individual increases, man exerts more and more control over his organic processes and becomes alienated from spontaneous behavior. His expression becomes "disembodied" and "ethereal." Douglas correlates this with religious norms concerning control of the body and consciousness and discusses the difference between religions of control and religions of ecstasy. In the former, strict ritual and behaviors are prescribed, whereas in the latter man is willing to surrender control of consciousness to achieve altered physical and mental states conducive to visions, spirit possession, or what worshippers simply call "getting the spirit." Examples include Pentecostal services, medieval mystics who experienced the bliss of Divine communion induced by fasting, or shamanic visions induced by ceremonial fasting and music.[18]

However, Douglas underestimates the degree to which devotees of ecstatic religions esteem the role of the body as an integral part of spirituality. She designates the ecstatic religions as lacking "magicality" or "symbolic expressions,"[19] even though many of these practices entail rich use of symbolism and ritual and are based on use of items imbued with magical properties, including the human body. Although Douglas interprets the ability to slide into altered states as an ability to disengage from the body and achieve a "disembodied" state, and the trance state certainly "disassociates" the participant from active control of his or her body, a larger integration is achieved. The possessed person merges with the cosmos of integrated material and spiritual harmony. One could also argue that the possessed person simply moves to a different level of awareness of this integration with the cosmos or spiritual world, which exists whether or not it is experienced as an "altered" state. A continuum of states of consciousness exists. Christianity stresses purposeful setting aside of desires and ego in order to perform good works and bear the fruit of one's faith. In some forms of ecstatic worship devotees may temporarily lose sense of themselves as autonomous individuals and lose control of their actions. In religious possession the personality of the devotee moves over so a deity spirit can inhabit his or her body. Although in the extreme of spirit possession, as Maya Deren points out "man and God cannot exist simultaneously," the trance state accomplishes "a state of timelessness and fusion with the world around us . . . ecstatic harmony with all being that cannot be further intellectualized."[20] Describing a similar state facilitated by psychedelic drugs, Timothy Leary explains it as a result of being able to relinquish not just personality but ego.[21] In a religious context, participants lose their autonomous, willful ego, but in return are infused with "the spirit." The individual as previously known temporarily does not exist. Instead a communion between the earthly human world and the spiritual world is achieved as the human body mediates between and integrates humankind and God. The human body becomes the ultimate magical talisman.

A willingness to admit communication between unseen cosmic energies and the tangible world is partially based in beliefs that objects once part of the same whole or related to one another retain a potent psychic connection when physically separated. Whatever happens to one part or object causes a sympathetic effect in the corresponding part.[22] This contagious magic involving the human body and spirit could be called "body magic." Any part of a person's body or any item in close contact with someone's body retains a powerful connection with that person. Examples include superstitious beliefs about hair, nail parings, spit, blood, and sweat. Because these physical residues are so intimately tied to the spirit, manipulation of them has repercussions and sympathetic effects on the person from whom they originate. A person wanting to cast a spell on someone need only procure a few strands of hair to obtain influential power over the person.[23] This magic also extends to physical images, such as face masks stylized to capture the essence of certain gods.

From here it is a small slide into symbolic representations. Thus, the Christian cross, a symbol made powerful by its intimate connection with Christ's physical suffering, can be considered a magical charm that protects the wearer against misfortune.

Many cultural customs, such as taking communion, the symbolic body of Christ, can be interpreted as rarefied body magic. When so-called primitive societies ate the bodies of their victims or ritual sacrifices, *they* were considered barbaric, whereas they were often practicing spiritual rituals. Aggressive forms of cannibalism were based on the belief that eating the flesh of one's victim would allow the eater to absorb the courage and spiritual power of the victim. Affectionate cannibalism relied on the same idea of body magic through body incorporation—that if one ate part of a deceased loved one it was a form of closeness, a commemoration, and way to keep the deceased, quite directly, a part of oneself. By taking into the body that which is loved, feared, or hated, one practices a form of body magic. Most societies that previously practiced cannibalism have replaced these practices of mourning and celebration with symbolic gestures. These gestures often rely on body magic such as marking the body or self-mutilation. Western society has further attenuated body magic practices that show grief or victory to outward gestures such as marking the body with ashes for Ash Wednesday, or wearing black at funerals, or eating a communion wafer.[24]

Western culture has gradually become aware that there is a connection between the mind and body and tentatively accepts technologies like biofeedback or Zen meditation. A small portion of the population explores the idea that manipulation of the body can open a person to spiritual insight by using T'ai Chi, yoga, Sufi dance, or breathing techniques to alter brain waves. Still, although analysis of changes in brain wave patterns can confirm altered consciousness and methods for measuring chemical levels in the bloodstream are becoming more sophisticated, science is lacking the ability to explain what happens beyond the detectable physical changes in the body. Systems of healing like acupuncture have not been explained by Western medicine, nor have the effects of many psychotropic drugs. Vibrations of drum rhythms help induce trance and spirit possession if the rhythm synchronizes with brain waves, but what possession is remains unknown. These phenomena, the "magic" of human energy in contact with other forces, are known only intuitively through the body. As a practitioner of Brazilian Macumba, in which individuals are possessed by spirits, says: "Macumba doesn't explain anything. . . . It is not practiced with the head but with the body."[25]

Crossing the boundary between the internal and external body is particularly powerful. Whenever the boundary between these two domains is crossed, the potential for body magic exists. Many societies consider body orifices targets for dangerous physical and spiritual contamination because they are sites of interaction with the external world.[26] Body fluids that cross body boundaries, such as spit and blood, are potent and sometimes feared sources of contamination because of their power to conduct invisible interactions between individuals and the cosmos. The body mutilations I discuss throughout this text are all acts of manipulating the body barrier, albeit in provocatively different ways. Anorectics refuse to consume matter foreign to their bodies. Bulimics consume and then forcefully expel food. Tattooees pierce their skin with needles that leave permanent pigmentation in the lowest layers of the epidermis. Body piercers stud their ears, septums, navels, eyebrows, nipples, and genitals with jewelry. Self-mutilators draw blood by cutting their wrists, arms, thighs, stomachs, breasts, and sometimes genitals.

The act of shedding blood is perhaps the most universally powerful example of crossing the barrier between the external and internal body. Although different cultures have different levels of alarm at seeing blood shed, all recognize bleeding as precious fluid leaving the body. As blood leaves an individual's body it loses its connection to the bleeder and acquires generic, universal status. "Blood has always symbolized the essence of life; it is 'considered to be the seat of the soul,' 'the Divine fluid' that maintains, nourishes and purifies incarnated life. It energizes the cells of the body by bringing nutrients and oxygen to every corner of our material being. It is the fluid that carries materialized energy."[27]

Blood is intimately connected with practices of body alteration, and is considered a sacred substance that is frequently used for religious purposes. Blood is important in Yoruban ritual ceremonies because it contains *ashe,* the potential to bring things into existence. This powerful life force, which exists in all things animate and inanimate, including the spoken word, is released when blood is spilled during ritual sacrifices. Animal blood is poured on ritual objects associated with deities to nurture the gods in exchange for protection and luck.[28] The Christian religion sanctifies Christ's blood as a "redeeming fluid which reunites man with God, i.e., the ego with the self."[29] Blood is associated with pain, injury, and the mystery of death, as well as with the enigmas of menstruation and childbirth. Many cultures have taboos concerning menstrual blood or menstruating women, although the global diversity of celebration and stigma concerning menstruation testifies to the differing contexts for different kinds of bloodshed. Fear of AIDS has caused blood and other body fluids to be thought of even more frequently as sources of possibly fatal contamination.

Evidence of body magic dates in cave paintings from 5000 B.C. of human figures that appear to be tattooed or scarred.[30] The British anthropologist W.D. Hambly, who published a comprehensive history of tattooing around the world in 1925, hypothesizes that the first body marking may have been the use of red ochre to symbolize the vitality of blood.[31] The very first body art that may be connected with magico-religious beliefs dates back to the Neanderthals covering bones with red ochre, which may have represented blood.[32] In 1991, mountaineers discovered the corpse of a prehistoric man in a glacier in the Austrian Alps. Because the body was so well preserved forensic experts detected that this man who had lived 5,000 years ago had had blue lines tattooed along his spine and on his feet and ankles, and a cross tattooed on the inside of his knee. X-rays showed that all of these tattooed sites suffered joint degeneration, leading the experts to postulate that the man had contracted for the tattoos as magical medicinal therapy.[33]

Many cultures, including our own, still practice various forms of body magic, although sometimes without awareness of the magical belief underlying the actions. Contemporary culture has attenuated many practices previously considered magical, religious, or spiritual into secular activities. The medical explanation of the danger of infection accounts rationally for our caution in handling spit, mucus, blood, and other body fluids, but cannot account for our irrational response of abhorrence to these substances. Our visceral reactions to body fluids betray our fear of destroying the unity of the human body. We recoil at the sight of blood, phlegm, or vomit. We are repulsed by someone spitting on the table. Yet we regard anyone who treats these bodily items as meaningful beyond their bacterial content as eccentric. We would call a person paranoid who hoarded nail parings to prevent them from falling into the hands of a hostile magician, or obsessive who collected the hairs of a lover in order to cast a love spell. Although we condone drug use to alter consciousness if the drug is legal, we look askance at a person who claims to have had a spiritual experience while under the influence of LSD, practitioners of Tantric sex or breathing rituals, or people who chant to reach enlightenment.

The Modern Magical Body

The intuitive spirituality of the body—and a spirituality that encompasses physical reality as well as unseen psychic energies, although based in ancient practices and beliefs, are gradually entering mainstream thought of the 1990s. The history of body alteration and the nuances of its various cultural and spiritual meanings would comprise a lifetime of research, but a brief introduction is essential to understanding contemporary shifts in attitude toward body alteration. During the Western peregrination toward modernity, ornamental and religious body marking and alteration became associated with pagan barbarism according to the European world view that dichotomized spirit and flesh and sought out reasons to degrade unfamiliar and colonized cultures. Ancient Egyptian culture located spirituality in physical existence, but by the time of Greek civilization the body was considered an inferior manifestation of a more noble and abstract perfect body. Augustine furthered a schism between man's physical and spiritual existence as he preached the sinfulness of sexual desire and the need to discipline the body. His influence extended through the middle ages and Anglo-European Christian culture began to see bodies as "interchangeable" and "non-essential"[34] to man's spiritual growth. Acceptance of magical and symbolic use of the body declined. Medieval practices of venerating relics—the preserved body parts of saints and mystics—faded.[35] Physical existence became something to be conquered in order to transcend one's humanness and become spiritual. Once the body and its desires were discarded, pure spirit could be achieved. Medieval saints who practiced chastity and ascetic activities that punished the body believed they were renouncing the body rather than enlisting it in the journey toward mystical union with God. This is in direct contrast to religious practices that consciously train the body to enter altered states and consider integrating body and mind an essential element of religious ecstasy.

Indian Tantrism, for example, rebels against the dualism that proposes asceticism as the path to enlightenment. The Tantric claim that bodily pleasure and spiritual reality coexist creates paths to enlightenment accessible to individuals not ordinarily credited with spiritual capabilities. As one of the Tantras explains, "Ananda (the mind-expanding bliss that is the essence of Reality and Self) is the form of the Brahman (the transcendental Self) and that Ananda is installed in the body."[36] By validating the body as a spiritual temple necessary to attain enlightenment in a single life-time, Tantric teachings during the eighth through twelfth centuries encouraged anyone from any social class to strive for spiritual knowledge.[37] The Tantric philosophy of embracing sexual desires and pleasure as a method of obtaining divine communion was, and remains, controversial. Likewise, the medieval mystics caused consternation in the church when they claimed to experience the bliss of divine union without the aid of scripture or church authorities by fasting and flagellating them-selves. While the saints may not have known they were democra-tizing spiritual bliss, the Catholic church probably did. This was probably the basis for Catholic castigation of many of the ascetic women mystics for their extreme and unauthorized practices.[38]

Christian sects have often encouraged women to suffer passively as an act of piety instead of actively attempting redemp-tion. The association between holiness and physical suffering has been especially potent metaphorically for women. The critical models for female suffering include the belief in God's infliction of painful childbirth upon by all women as punishment for Eve's folly of eating the serpent's apple, and the suffering of the Virgin Mary as she saw her holy son crucified. The former epitomizes female suffering as punishment for sin, the latter is a supreme act of suffering as proof of piety, second only to Christ's submission to crucifixion. These models enforce the dimension of submissive-ness in the Christian view of physical suffering. The Puritans who came to the New World found this passive acceptance especially appealing as a metaphor for piety, as discussed by Amanda Porterfield. She argues persuasively, however, that during the period of the Salem witch trials, bodily suffering came to connote satanic affliction rather than holiness.[39] One more avenue to the heavens had been demolished. Mankind was now left in a double bind. Indulging in sensory pleasure was base, yet to suffer was the work of the Devil. Perhaps it was best to ignore the body alto-gether, and deny both its pains and pleasures.

Discussing contemporary views of the body, philosopher Susan Bordo comments: "[T]o my students the body is the enemy, to be beaten into submission."[40] Many individuals, in many different ways, struggle with the split between spirit and body and try to reconcile the seemingly two entities into a singular symbiotic whole. Based on his treatment of patients with eating disorders, John Sours observes that his patients see the body "as a thing to be controlled and not indulged. It is a despicable threat and not an object of pleasure or beauty."[41] This attitude is not such a far cry from "normal" cultural views that seek to mold the body into acceptable standards of beauty and thinness.

Modern cultural taboos concerning the human body are grounded not only in rational fears of physical and spiritual contamination, but in the Western concept of a dichotomy between a "natural" body and the body that culture civilizes.[42] The body has been a battleground for spiritual and moral issues for centuries. The "natural" body opposes the intellectual mind and is relegated to the field of natural sciences. By refuting the idea that the body is nothing more than coarse organic tissue and functional systems, the modern humanities can include the body in discussions of culture and history. Academic scholarship has explored racism, sexism, media images of the body, laws governing use and abuse of the body, implications of health care and sexual norms, treatment of the body in literature and other texts, and the body as the ground for power struggles. Academics have expended less energy analyzing the physical reality of the body as text, especially spiritual text.

In a culture where we lack shared meaningful rituals, cohesive values, or a clear passage from childhood to adulthood the human body has taken on greater significance. Spread across looming billboards to advertise beer and splayed out on tanning beds across the nation, our bodies and other people's fascinate us. As a culture we are obsessed with titillation, sensations, and feeling alive. As Philip Rieff comments, "A social structure shakes with violence and shivers with fears of violence not merely when that structure is callously unjust, but also when its members must stimulate themselves to feverish activity in order to demonstrate how alive they are."[43] In an increasingly secularized and fragmented American culture, we incessantly search for something to satisfy our desires and help us define ourselves and the meaning of our daily lives.

We turn to the body because it cannot be denied. We get old, we die, we disintegrate into dust, but our living bodies are proof of our here-and-now existence in a world that is too often numb

and confusing. In our mental gymnastics we choreograph physical existence, while we attempt to revitalize our daily life. In a
tightening economic climate that augments competitive attitudes,
we expend increasing amounts of energy on our health, how we
look, and how we function according to perceived standards and
expectations. Advances in medicine have encouraged us to
believe that the body is perfectible and preservable. The cultural
shift of the 1960s and 1970s encouraged less rigid restriction of
sexuality, while the subsequent threat of AIDS requires caution
when engaging in sexual liaisons. Shifts in attitudes toward the
body are circumstantial, rapid, and complex.

A shift in earlier attitudes toward bodily habits is explored by
Norbert Elias in his documentation of the development of standardized manners. In *The Civilizing Process: The History of
Manners*, Elias credits Erasmus with first documenting a relation
between human bodily habits and the inner, spiritual self. In the
late 1400s and early 1500s Erasmus ushered in "psychological
observation,"[44] in which humanity began to self-analyze and
judge spiritual value according to social conduct. Instead of
producing a happy collusion between physical, social, and spiritual existence, this vigilance of behavior placed humanity in the
position of controlling bodily impulses, and created a tension
between private and social behavior. With the burgeoning of the
aristocracy, individuals became self-conscious of social class as
reflected by an aesthetic of bodily discipline.

The rise of an aristocratic class led to court manners and codi-
fied distinctions between the classes according to dress and
behavior. The aesthetic of self-control gradually crept into
everyday life as the "civilizing process" encouraged people to
subdue their natural impulses to touch, sniff, scratch, slurp, and
satisfy other pleasures.[45] Social hierarchy dictated rules for
exposing the body. For example, upper-class men and women
could appear naked or perform intimate hygienic tasks in front of
individuals of inferior social status. "Shame" as Elias notes "is a
social function molded by social structure."[46] As manners became
what in part demarcated a person's social standing, shame about
the body and its natural functions increased accordingly. Elias's
discussion establishes the conflation between manipulation of the
body and social status in Western culture.

More recently, feminist theory, the gay rights movement, and
holistic health models have sought to integrate the human body
with human identity.[47] The new paradigms recognize that phys-

ical health holds the hand of mental health. Activists for women's rights are seeking enhanced vitality through proper health care, reproductive rights, and working conditions. The body is being reclaimed as an ally in self-expression, and the forefront of the gay rights movement strives for the right to claim sexual behavior and identity with impunity. The body and physical desires are sometimes celebrated, but we still struggle with beliefs that the body should be standardized and conquered. Individuals manipulate their bodies as a method of recreating themselves through harsh diet regimes, unrealistically strenuous exercise, plastic surgery, and more recently tattooing and body piercing. The difference between *expression of* and *masking of* identity is fiercely debated in feminist discourse as critics denounce body alteration, and proponents praise it as self-expression. These issues even enter the discourse about race relations in America as various critics applaud or denigrate Michael Jackson for altering his skin, hair, and facial features in order, according to some critics, to appear more Caucasian.

One element of this reclamation of the body is its underlying narcissism. While rejecting the idea that the gaze of another defines us, we cannot escape the defining gaze or cease objectifying our own bodies. Although the idea of self-creation is not new, today it is more pervasive than ever. Christopher Lasch claims that in contemporary society our daily lives are saturated with self-absorption and self-construction. He succinctly notes that "life becomes a work of art."[48] Narcissist concern with the role image plays in success is compelling more and more people to consider their bodies the artistic canvas upon which they will construct their ideal identity. Sometimes consciously, sometimes unconsciously, the body has become a retreat for personal, social, and spiritual identity.

Body Narcissism

Body perception is a large part of identity formation, and many factors contribute to a person's image of his or her own body. Saturated by images of youthful, seemingly perfect professional models and their lithe bodies, few individuals, especially women, do not experience some sort of dissatisfaction at some time or another with their physical being. An abbreviated survey of the history of fashion shows a long tradition of changing the appearance of the body according to culturally sanctioned standards of beauty. The inflictions humans have endured (and still endure) to appear more alluring and acceptable range from simple and temporary, to humiliating and permanently deforming. A brief list might include shaving, tweezing, dyeing, bleaching, wearing false teeth, false eyelashes, high heels, corsets, and hobble skirts, cicatrization (scarification), tattooing, skull shaping, and foot binding, not to mention surgical reconstruction of the body.

Describing the body as the oldest artistic medium, Bernard Rudofsky points out that mankind is the only species that has the desire to alter his body. Rudofsky attributes this to a vain desire to look better and prime the ego. Humans wish to transcend the imperfection of nature, which "demands more than artistry or resemblance; in fact resemblance may be the last thing [human-kind] wants. To shore up his ego, he needs an icon, a holy picture of his inner self. Only a faultlessly constructed mask will meet his need—and his approval."[49] Striving to adorn and improve nature proposes the human creative and spiritual superiority to animals. Religion serves a similar function. This explains why so many acts of body alteration have magical and spiritual connotations.

Although Rudofsky does not address the physical conse-quences of body alteration, he does consider various physical and psychological functions of clothing. He theorizes that clothing is not only a mentally and spiritually satisfying method of trans-forming, or at least masking, the self, but that clothing is a form of self-touch. Apart from protection from environmental hazards, clothing provides tactile pleasure: warmth, softness, comforting constriction, and other forms of autoeroticism. The physical and emotional pleasures of adornment are "narcissistic and exhibi-tionist pleasures."[50] The same is true for body alteration as a form of self-touch. A discussion of narcissism will illuminate how "self-touch" may be imbued with emotional, magical, and spiritual meaning.

Pathological narcissism is called a disorder of the self because narcissistic individuals have so much difficulty distinguishing the boundaries between themselves and the external world that thay are unable to maintain a firm notion of identity. Because narcis-sistic individuals lack a cohesive self, they are incessantly strug-gling to create and confirm an identity and a sense of continuity by relating to "self-objects" that mirror themselves and confirm their self-worth. These self-objects may be other people, or they may be physical objects that the narcissist manipulates to secure a psychological and physical confirmation of existence. Because one of the ways in which a child forms a sense of self as a whole and separate entity is by being held and handled, skin contact is an essential part of recognizing boundaries of the self and interacting with the external world. Without sufficient handling and sensory stimulation a child may grow up to have low self-esteem and a distorted body image.[51] Such an individual may learn to use his or her body and its physical sensations as a solacing, "transitional object," an object that replaces the childhood caretaker's task of confirming a bounded self apart from an external world.

Although I have used the term *disorder* it is important to recognize the ambiguity of this term. Physical being is important to all individuals, especially during certain developmental stages or times of pleasure or sickness, and at one time or another we all comfort ourselves with certain foods, clothing, music, or even smells that reinstate psychological stability by providing physical pleasure. As Heinz Kohut says, "[I]ntegrity of the body self is a prevalent content of the nuclear self."[52] Adolescents typically view the body as a transitional object for a period during their development, but narcissistic individuals experience difficulty moving beyond this stage.[53] This is typical of individuals with eating disorders who often have a distorted image of their bodies.

The narcissist simultaneously seeks to "be self" and paradoxically "not to be self." The narcissist wants his or her existence confirmed, but simultaneously wants to escape the dreadful pain of being an individual alone and unconnected to any other being in the cosmos. The narcissistic anxiety and fear of disintegration can only be eased by identifying with, subsuming, and being subsumed by, an Other. This overbearing, unhealthy desire for an unreachable and perfect unity is an exaggeration of a very normal human desire for something stable and predictable. In some instances, if this stability is not provided by a family or community milieu, an individual may depend upon private rituals for security, or learn that he or she can only find solace in predictable physical stimuli. The searching individual may find comfort in ritualized sadomasochistic interactions or an attachment to a self-object, such as his or her body.[54]

Narcissists both reject and cherish their bodies. "The corruptible aspects of the body—illness, aging, and death—frighten the narcissist." The narcissistic attempts to surmount the limitations of the body in order to deny change and mortality. Because extreme narcissists so desperately desire something they can trust, they believe that the "ego should be above the body's natural fate, it should be unchanging, indestructible, and deathless."[55] Physical sensation may become unusually meaningful for an individual with a disorder of the self and may be manifested in an acute sensitivity to skin eroticism, including both painful and pleasurable sensations. "For an individual without a distinct body image or with a regressive fragmentation of the self, pain can be a means of creating a feeling of aliveness and realness. The receipt of pain establishes or reestablishes a boundary—an experience of existing as a bounded, contained entity."[56] To feel is to be. Many of the actions discussed here are painful methods of creating or reestablishing a sense of self.

Individuals with a fragmented sense of self confirm and delineate their body boundaries (and therefore the boundaries of their psychological self) by various forms of skin and body stimulation. They may obsessively wear particular kinds of clothes to feel the material and sensation of rubbing, cut or maim their skin, or compulsively engage in sex. Bingeing, vomiting, and using laxatives or diuretics also cause physical body sensations that shock the body.[57] Even exercise may be a pathological expression of the need to feel bounded. "The frenetic pace of excruciating exercise, running, and swimming characteristic of the anorectic may appear to be for the purpose of losing weight, but it is actually a desperate attempt to experience the reality of their bodies, for which they do not have an accurate or distinct mental representation. It is also an effort (as is controlled eating, or of vomiting) at countering the anguish of internal emptiness, boredom, and deadness."[58]

If, as Philip Cushman claims, individuals in contemporary society are perceiving a diminished capacity to be "masterful and bounded,"[59] it is no surprise that more and more individuals are experimenting with "skin eroticism" and turning to their bodies as frontiers for establishing a sense of spiritual and social identity. Although Mary Douglas contends that the more tightly a social structure controls an individual, the more control an individual relinquishes over his or her conduct and body, the contemporary trend of body alteration appears to be a rebellious struggle to regain a grounded sense of self, and achieve the narcissistic paradox of individuation and yet integration into a spiritual and subcultural cradle that will impart a feeling of social and spiritual identity.

2

Pain as a Pathway to Social and Spiritual Identity

Body and Spirit

In *Pain and Religion* Steven Brena presents a definition of religion that I will use to define spirituality.

> True living religion could be the conscious self-effort to
> bind together in ever-expanding states of consciousness of the
> body, the mind, and the soul toward the bliss of God-commu-
> nion.[1]

Spiritual practices attempt to achieve a balanced interaction between believers and the cosmic forces that affect them. Religious and spiritual beliefs acknowledge the power of cosmic forces—whether called God or Nature—and yet attempt to achieve some level of communication with them and implicitly believe that humankind can influence them with certain behaviors. Religion seeks an integration of humankind and divine forces, whether by achieving Nirvana as a final stage of reincarnation, getting into Heaven to be in God's grace, or being possessed by a deity. When this integration is achieved, the believer feels a harmony of mind, body, and soul, and a wholeness with divine forces. Brena promotes prayer as a path toward this goal of cosmic unity, and claims disciplined prayer empowers the devotee to rise above sensory experiences and become obedient to "moral duties and intuitive wisdom."[2] Meditation and prayer evoke a feeling of harmony with the universe and enable the practitioner to pursue spiritual goals. Although Brena claims that prayer behaviors are the opposite of what he calls "pain behaviors," upon closer examination many similarities exist between their functions.

Like intense pleasure, pain may result in a feeling of harmony between mind, body, and spirit. Pain can prompt a loss of awareness of the self or ego, or in contradiction, acutely mark one's physical existence and result in awareness of one's precise place in the universe. Both processes may be analogous to a spiritual experience of union with the cosmos. Without promoting self-infliction of pain as a spiritual activity, this chapter will examine the quest for spiritual union through ascetic behaviors and self-inflicted pain as ways to simultaneously confirm the self and escape the self. I will argue that all of these actions are attempts to fulfill the universally human desire to locate oneself in a social and/or spiritual milieu.

Aldous Huxley believed that the desire to transcend "self-conscious selfhood . . . is a principal appetite of the soul," and observed that

> if men and women torment their bodies, it is not only because they hope in this way to atone for past sins and avoid future punishments, it is also because they long to visit the mind's antipode and do some visionary sightseeing. Empirically and from the reports of other ascetics, they know that fasting and a restricted environment will lead them where they long to go. Their self-inflicted punishment may be the door to paradise.

Huxley pointed out that self-flagellation promotes the release of histamines and adrenaline into the bloodstream, which may lead to a physiologically based mystical experience. If the wounds are left to fester, the body may release toxic substances to ward off infection, and these chemicals may cause hallucinations.[3]

Perhaps the basis of many spiritual experiences is physiological. Ancient and not so ancient religions and mystics seem to have intuitively understood what science is only now beginning to theorize about—the role of the body in psychological states. Huxley's ideas were based in part on his study of religions and in part on his experiences with drugs that alter brain chemistry. In the 1970s, when biochemists discovered opiate receptors in the body, they developed a more sophisticated model of how the body reacts to pain and injury. Although the range and variations of physiological responses to physical pain and emotional distress are complicated and beyond the scope of this book, a brief description is necessary to understand what physiological effects self-mutilation might incur. The act of self-mutilation, whether it is the benign act of piercing an eyebrow or getting a tattoo, or the act of damaging the body by repeatedly inducing vomiting or cutting the skin, is a complex physical and psychological event.

The act of traumatizing one's flesh is accompanied by a variety of emotional states such as nervousness, anger, excitement, fear, sadness, frustration, and perhaps disassociation.

According to the belief that mind and body are integrated, the cause-effect model of sensation followed by physical response or emotion followed by physical response is simplistic, but provides a touchstone for a discussion of physiology. For the moment I will omit ideas about mankind's ability to control physiological response to consider what generally happens in the body when someone feels emotional or physical distress. The physiological responses of the body vary in intensity according to the intensity of the sensation experienced. When an individual becomes suddenly angry, frightened, or excited, he or she experiences a "flight-or-fight" response in which the body conserves energy for functions that may be needed for immediate survival. Adrenaline is released into the bloodstream causing respiration and heartbeat to quicken. Muscles tense, blood pressure and blood sugar rise, and blood flow to the heart, skin, lungs, and muscles increases. Responses to less urgent stress are similar, but are triggered by cortisol, which is a slower acting chemical.[4] While in a state of excitement an individual is less likely to notice and react to physical pain.[5]

Although less likely to feel pain, the distressed person's body reacts to the shock of injury. Certain combinations of amino acids that form peptide neurotransmitters, also called neuropeptides, swarm into the bloodstream. These natural chemicals: endorphins, enkephalins, and dynorphin, bind to opiate receptors in the brain and throughout the body and trigger a series of physiological events that induce narcotic effects like drowsiness and pain inhibition.[6] Candace Pert, a biochemist who helped discover opiate receptors, theorizes that because neuropeptides travel via the bloodstream to receptors throughout the body they integrate the body and unite mind/body communication (qtd. in Dienstfrey). For example, because the body is a network, it is not simply the mind that perceives a gut feeling of fear. The fear *is* perceived in the stomach. The receptors throughout the body and brain—not just the brain and its receptors—*is* the mind system. Emotions affect the body and the body affects emotions. Breathing changes, for example, can invoke mood changes by altering the neuropeptide flow throughout the body[7] and sending the body/mind network messages of either calmness if the breathing is regular and tranquil, or panic if the breathing is quick and shallow.

Although the exact effects of the opiate-like neuropeptides have not been delineated, they have been linked to mood and behavior changes, mental health, and pain inhibition.[8]

Certain foods, or abstinence from food, also cause changes in mental and emotional states, ranging from mood elevation to hallucinations. Some people may be particularly susceptible to certain foods, and may develop caffeine or sugar addictions. Carbohydrates can also be addictive due to their tranquilizing effects.[9] Other foods, such as hot peppers, may produce physical euphoria.[10] Prolonged abstinence from food precipitates changes in consciousness and cognitive malfunctions. A starving individual often becomes preoccupied with internal thought processes and physical sensations and loses touch with external time and reality. Anorectics often reach a euphoric feeling of transcendence. "You feel outside your body. You are truly beside yourself—and then you are in a different state of consciousness and you can undergo pain without reacting. That's what I did with hunger," claims one anorectic.[11] Altered states of consciousness due to extreme malnutrition and starvation may have been responsible for many of the medieval religious visions.[12] Native Americans used the physiological and psychological effects of fasting to produce visions during the three-day Vision Quest. John the Baptist experienced his revelations while restricting himself to locusts and honey in the desert. Judaic and Islamic rituals include less extreme fasting to commemorate or celebrate religious events.

Throughout history, humans have inflicted physical discomfort and suffering upon themselves, not only for aesthetic reasons but in the name of religion and the desire to feel part of some kind of cosmic order. The discomfort may range from simple celibacy which many religions encourage as a matter of moral or holy virtue, to "radical spiritual cure[s]" that entail harsh endurance tests, "injury, pain, and inhumanity."[13] Plains Indian warriors who withstood the physical ordeal of the Sun Dance, in which they were skewered with wooden sticks, expected to receive mystical visions. This ritual was similar to the Mandan Indian Oh-Kee-Pa ceremony in which warriors were hung from hooks in their skin. The history of Christianity is replete with accounts of self-sacrifice and self-torture. Shaman mythology abounds with acts of self-mutilation.[14]

In *The Varieties of Religious Experience*, William James noted both the punitive and redemptive functions of self-inflicted pain and asceticism. James discusses asceticism as both a sacrifice "to purge out sin, and buy safety" and as a "spontaneous impulse . . . for the pure love of God."[15] James discusses the fourteenth-century German mystic Suso, whose self-tortures included wearing a hair shirt, wearing an iron chain that cut his skin, driving sharp tacks into his skin, and wearing an undergarment with sharp nails fixed in it that would pierce his flesh. James calls Suso an example of "the irrational extreme to which a psychopathic individual may go in the line of body austerity," without realizing that Suso may have transported himself to an endorphin-induced euphoric state in which he felt a blissful union with God.[16] Shaman scholar Holger Kalweit describes this state as dissolving the differences between mind and matter, inner and outer world, through a process of disabling "all the mechanisms that maintain a stable ego fixed on the events of the external world."[17] Suso may have developed a keen awareness of himself as a powerful individual because of his ability to master his pain and discomfort. As he reached an endorphin-induced euphoria he may have experienced dissolution of his ego and experienced not only mystical visions but a narcissistic sense of the self as united with a larger being. Considering Candace Pert's incomplete but provocative theory that neuropeptides circulating in the body integrate the mind and body systems, the mystical feeling of divine union may well be a physiological as well as psychological experience.

The most famous example of mortification of the flesh in order to achieve cosmic union is when Jesus is nailed to the cross. At the moment Jesus suffers this crucifixion, he is experiencing intense physical pain of human dimension, but is paradoxically transcending his physical being and commencing his journey toward heaven. Willfully suffering crucifixion not only marks Christ as superior to animals, but as superior to human beings. The crucifixion epitomizes the experience of pain as a pathway to spiritual transformation.

Pain and Transcendence of the Self

Many contradictions exist in the experience of pain. When one experiences intense pain, one becomes acutely aware of physical existence and loses rational cognition. An individual in extreme pain may lose the ability to think or speak. Conversely, to be able to withstand pain is to transcend one's physical limits and become closer to a spiritual realm of being. Pain can both reaffirm an individual's physical existence and aliveness, and provoke a transcendence of this existence.

Pain as a potent vehicle of power and mastery can obliterate and recreate consciousness. Pain inflicted without consent negates the sufferer's integrity, but self-inflicted pain can bestow dignity and sense of self, and also provoke a feeling of connection with something beyond one's self boundaries. The sufferer experiences sensations that cannot be shared and that separate him or her from others, which may induce a profound awareness of physical limits and emotional solitude.[18] Conversely, pain may also provide an escape from one's separateness. A person in acute pain becomes oblivious to everything but the present moment and loses self-awareness and high-level thinking. Psychological studies of masochism reveal that a masochist uses pain to "lose awareness of his or her normal everyday self."[19] Pain may be experienced as a loss of boundaries between self and environment that evokes a feeling of union with something beyond mortal earthly existence. If not experienced in this spiritual way, it may be experienced as being acutely in touch with the surrounding environment, and even identifying with the source of pain. This is especially true when people inflict pain upon themselves. They are simultaneously merging with, and differentiating themselves from the environment. Consenting to pain may provide a similar experience.

One of the motives for sadomasochistic activity is "loss of personhood,"[20] which is concurrent with the repair of a narcissistic fragmented self and alleviation of the accompanying emotional distress. This may be true for either the person who receives pain or who inflicts pain, neither of whom may have any kind of narcissistic disorder of the self, but wish to experience the psychological and physiological euphoria induced by their actions. Some individuals who practice sadomasochism claim that pain takes them or their partners into physical and spiritual realms of bliss. Commenting on the ability of pain to alter consciousness, one practicing sadomasochist says, "Your body releases endorphins and it's better than any high I've obtained doing drugs."[21] The same interviewee entertains the consideration that the euphoria produced by pain may be addicting. Research shows that the brain may block transmission of pain signals if other strong sensory stimulation (for example, sexual stimulation) is experienced at the same time.[22] A discussion of ritualized acts of sadomasochism provides an fertile ground to explore the idea that physiological and psychological events can fulfill a need for confirmation of the self, while also providing an avenue to transcend the self. Although all acts of sadomasochism are unique, and no two individuals who practice these acts are moved by the same impetus, the idea of transcendence of the self is a useful tool to analyze the significance of acts of consentual sadomasochism, domination and submission, and bondage and discipline. All use the body, most rely on elements of ritual, and all seek to establish and break boundaries of the self, boundaries between the participants, and in some cases, boundaries between the participants and the cosmos. Abolishing these boundaries may result in Brena's experience of "ever-expanding states of consciousness of the body, the mind, and the soul toward the bliss of God-communion." Although the labels sadomasochism, bondage and discipline, and dominance and submission carry different connotations and imply different practices, I will use the terms *sadomasochistic* and *sadomasochism* as generic terms indicating activities that revolve around physically expressing a role-play of status disparity. Although not all of these forms necessarily involve pain, most involve some degree of physical discomfort inflicted upon the participant who assumes the subordinate role. The activities may or may not be sexual in nature.

In a provocative essay Jessica Benjamin examines sadomasochist interactions as both a confirmation and escape from self. Based on Hegel's discussion of the master-slave relationship, Benjamin asserts that acts of dominance and submission rely on interdependence between the dominator and the dominated for recognition. In her discussion of *The Story of O,* a novel that presents sadomasochistic scenarios in which the main character, O, submits to her lover's sadistic wishes, Benjamin concludes that "pain is the violent rupture of self-organization," while it is simultaneously an attempt to affirm a sense of self. "O finds a kind of substitute transcendence in losing herself to enslavement." O hopes that by submitting to pain she will be brought to life by the recognition of her torturer and through the awakening of her senses, but also hopes to lose her boundaries by experiencing pain.

> She . . . experiences her lover as a god whom she adores and cannot stand to be parted from. While God represents the ultimate oneness, the ability to stand alone, O represents the lost soul who is elevated by union with the ideal omnipotent other.

Similar to a sexual experience, O's union with another individual is intimately connected with body sensation in her process of self-definition and awareness.[23] Benjamin's trenchant contribution is her analysis of submission to pain as a method of gaining recognition and self-confirmation. Although she does not mention the ability of pain to integrate the self via body chemistry, the physiological reactions to pain are relevant because of their ability to produce euphoria and feelings of narcotic wholeness and connectedness to others or the cosmos. Practitioners of Tantric sex rituals use prolonged pleasure for the same purpose. Individuals who endure the pain of nipple clamps, the discomfort of restraint, the sting of repeated whippings, or various other sadomasochistic activities may not experience severe pain, but may feel the effects of endorphins released in the body in reaction to prolonged discomfort. Individuals who experiment with erotic cutting, in which one partner cuts the other, or other extreme forms of sadomasochistic sex play, may experience more extreme endorphin thrills, and more intimate feelings of being connected to their partners. The clandestine and sexual pleasure that may accompany the activities may also provide psychological and physiological confirmation of identity as an individual, as part of a dyad, and as part of a secret community labeled deviant by mainstream society.

Identity as a dialectic between being separate from others and yet recognized and confirmed by them is expressed by the psychologist Edward Podvall in an article about self-mutilation. Identity is "on the one hand, a mere reflection . . . of the impinging social and cultural forces, and on the other, being uniquely and idiosyncratically separate and private from other minds."[24] The submission to pain highlights the private nature of self-awareness, while also providing a way to feel a connection with an external cause of sensation. In sadomasochistic interactions, inflicting pain and receiving pain are simultaneously private experiences and experiences that are witnessed and recognized by another. As the master or mistress dominates the submissive, he or she is assured of his or her sex appeal, self-worth, and self-mastery. The dominator regulates expression of his or her own desires as well as the behavior of the submissive. The subordinant participant functions as a crucial witness or "self-object" who confirms the dominator's self-control and power. Without a slave to manipulate, the master/mistress remains without an identity. Although widely considered deviant, the dominant-submissive play can be interpreted as a stylization of natural human desires to confirm one's own potency—as experienced by the dominator, and one's own importance in the face of a powerful force—as experienced by the submissive. When performed with affection and consent, human instincts of love and aggression merge as both partners willfully play out universal acts of domination, aggression, submission, and worship in a contained atmosphere. They confirm their own humanity as they exercise the will to choose their actions.

Many factors contribute to consensual acts of sadomasochism as ways to transcend the self and experience a feeling of cosmic connectedness. In an age when "safe sex" is a necessary precaution against sexually transmitted diseases, sadomasochism may carry an aura of danger, even though it can be practiced as safely as any other sexual activity, or perhaps more safely if body fluids are not exchanged. The feeling of transcending the danger of sex implies a transcendence of mortality and a god-like immunity to harm. As fashion theorist Valerie Steele points out, the fashions of sadomasochism and fetishism, leather, rubber, tight garments, garments reinforced with metal, heighten awareness of the body as bounded and purposefully controlled. As she claims, "[F]etish materials dramatize the exterior (boundary) aspects of the body. Fetish fashion draws attention to the sexual aspects of the body, while simultaneously restricting access to it."[25] Being snugly bound in a corset, rubber stockings, or thigh-high boots is a highly skin-erotic experience, as is being restrained in a leather collar, and ankle and wrist cuffs. The clothing adds to the transgressive fantasy of well-defined roles by making each participant feel literally physically defined and bounded, and therefore, safe.

When the interaction is ritualized, as it often is, the ritual may prepare the participants psychologically for a spiritual experience by gradually preparing a sacred atmosphere, a space and time set aside from the normal world of everyday life. As the participants don their special clothes and accouterments—for many of these rituals revolve around external appearance and special props or "toys"—they enter a different state of mind. Dressing, or being dressed by, one's partner becomes a passage into an arena in which both participants must follow certain rules. Not only do these rules provide a comforting feeling of security and predictability, but because they encourage behavior that is not normally acceptable in other arenas they allow the participants the freedom to act outside of themselves. As the mistress or master assumes her or his typically elaborate and expensive gear[26] and the slave accepts the slave collar, each individual enters a role. The master's whip and the slave's collar become masks that allow each to experience the "sacred awe" of both his or her own role and the role of the partner. The physical and psychological masks contribute to the creative disassociation from ordinary life. Like religious masks that facilitate altered states of consciousness, the masks of these roles allow the participants to transcend their own inhibitions and identities. As they experience the psychological and physical effects of pain and sexual pleasure, they may also experience themselves and each other as transcending their humanity. As they act out rituals of stylized domination and submission, and enter altered states of being, they may even experience themselves and each other as embodying universal forces traditionally labeled masculine and feminine, active and passive, Yin and Yang. Like the narcissistic use of a "self-object" to both create and transcend the ego, the participants use each other and each other's bodies to confirm and escape their identities and experience a feeling of integration with the cosmos. The experience of pain, the recognition by the other, and the escape from self culminate in what many practitioners of sadomasochistic activities describe as a spiritual experience.

The significance of pain depends on both its experience and its functional end result. Social institutions may inflict pain for utilitarian, symbolic, or expressive purposes.[27] The disparity between pain that is culturally sanctioned and pain inflicted by an individual transgressing social norms, whether publicly or in private, is salient to the interpretation of acts of self-mutilation. This disparity will be explored further in discussion of specific acts of self-inflicted pain. To indicate the continuum between these two extremes, I will discuss how marking the body functions in cultural rituals and several acts of self-mutilation that illustrate the continuum between pathology and social acceptability.

Marking the Body: Fulfilling a Ritual Promise
Throughout history humans have performed rituals to create order and predictability in an uncertain world. Rituals are idiographic proof of a value system. In his critique of American culture Robert Bellah claims, "We cannot know who we are without some practical ritual and moral 'structure' that orders our freedom and binds our choices."[28] Although Bellah is not referring to actual temporal and spatial rituals, his statement acknowledges

the analogy between rituals and moral codes that circumscribe social order. In the multicultural, competitive, often confusing American culture of religious pluralism, changing gender roles, MTV, racial tension, fast food, commercialism, increasing violence, and virtual reality, few formal national cultural rituals remain. Paradoxically, ritualistic activity permeates society. Americans enter spaces set apart for special purposes, such as drinking, eating, and learning; prepare to pass driving examinations as imputed initiation into an adult world of mobility; and celebrate holidays with traditional foods and gifts. Some of these structured activities are recognized as rituals and some are not.

Initiation rituals provide a structure for individuals to achieve a unique identity while becoming integrated into a social order. Discussing the lack of rituals of initiation in contemporary society, Joseph Henderson asserts that

> since modern man cannot return to his origins in any collective sense, he apparently is tempted and even forced to return to them in an individual way at certain critical times in his development, and in this resides the relevance today of re-informing ourselves of the nature of primitive forms of initiation.[29]

In a short story by Francis Amery, the narrator notes that "the purpose of ritual is to dignify an event and thus transform it into something more significant, something more meaningful. . . . [T]hrough ritual the tawdry becomes noble, the ordinary becomes extraordinary, and the mundane becomes supernatural."[30] If modern society does not provide viable rituals to achieve this transformation, individuals will create their own methods of initiation.

In spite of national holidays, American ideology seems to struggle with the finality of achieving the noble, the extraordinary, the supernatural, or the spiritual. Individuals struggle with achieving adult identity, let alone an extraordinary existence or even a definitive place within the social order. Although lack of space does not permit a thorough discussion of the fragmentation and alienation of modern American life, a quote from David Napier will evince the dilemma of the American ideology.

> Our "personhood" is less achieved through periodic rites of passage, in which the self is regularly redefined; rather we live in a constant state of redefinition . . . unity is for us . . . a covert

category, one that we do not emphasize even if it governs us all the same. Democratic as we are, we cling to the cult of individual.[31]

As we resist definition, we incessantly recreate ourselves. As we resist communal strictures, we are stuck in a constant state of becoming. A discussion of ritual will illuminate the significance of this state.

The anthropologist Arnold Van Gennep theorizes that every ritual ensures a transition from one mode of being to another. Structurally, every ritual is a rite of passage with three stages: an act of separation from previous status or identity; a transitory stage, which Van Gennep calls the "liminal," which is a preparation for the resolution that takes place in the final stage. Often this ritual process achieves a transition from childhood to adulthood. In many tribal or small-scale societies specific ceremonies exist to accomplish this passage.[32]

In the liminal stage the initiate is symbolically devoid of all identity and kin status, and often relinquishes adornment, clothes, and other social differentiation as well. The "liminal entity," as Victor Turner calls the initiate, is humble, obedient, and submissive, and accepts punishment without question. Blindfolded, kept in darkness and silence, the liminal entity is anonymous and passive while awaiting the bestowal of a new niche in the social order. In this anonymous state the initiate represents a state of nothingness, while simultaneously representing an chaotic melange of everything. The entity in transition takes on no role, all roles, and is bisexual, asexual, androgenous, amorphous, and undefinable. Metaphorically, the liminal stage is being in the womb, invisible, existing in wilderness and ambiguity.[33] Returning to the model of sadomasochistic interactions, one can easily compare the initiate who awaits social status to the slave who submissively awaits confirmation of identity from the master or mistress. Both in initiation rituals and sadomasochistic activities sensory deprivation has the power to alter body awareness and perception of reality, and to disorient an individual's sense of ego and self.[34]

Marking the body signifies the end of the liminal stage. In this final stage the initiate accepts social and adult identity, which is often confirmed by indelible scars or tattoos upon the initiate's body. The marks are often upon parts of the body that are essential to communication.[35] Mary Douglas asserts that religious rites promise to make some change in external events, and often invoke the potency of body fluids and boundaries as symbols of society.[36] The same is often true for secular rituals. Drawing blood and conferring a scar or other permanent mark upon the body fulfills the promise of external change. Approaching the efficacy of ritual from a holistic view that mind and body, and spiritual and physical worlds are inseparable, the resulting body alteration is not a one-dimensional external change, but a multidimensional fulfillment of the ritual promise.

Marking the body in a cultural ritual changes the position of the individual within the social structure. Van Gennep posits:

> cutting off, splitting, or mutilating any part of the body (modifies) the personality of the individual in a way visible to all . . . cutting off the foreskin is exactly equivalent to pulling out a tooth (Australia), to cutting off a little finger above the last joint (South Africa), to cutting off the earlobe or perforating the earlobe or septum, or to tattooing, scarifying, or cutting the hair in a particular fashion. The mutilated individual is removed from the common mass of humanity by a rite of separation (this is the idea behind cutting, piercing, etc.) which automatically incorporates him into a defined group, since the operation leaves ineradicable traces, the incorporation is permanent.[37]

Altering the body not only incurs a specific social status, it signifies "man's paradoxical identity with and separation from the animal world."[38] Marking the body as a culmination of a culturally sanctioned initiation ritual is a signature of socialization.

The use of pain in sadomasochistic interactions is process-oriented and relies on pain to provoke awareness of body boundaries and self, while also using pain to obliterate the ego and promote a feeling of transcendence and connection with the cosmos. A second method is both process-oriented and product-oriented. Through a culturally sanctioned ritual an initiate transforms from a liminal entity to a defined and physically marked individual within the social structure. Anorexia, self-cutting, tattooing, and piercing are similar to these methods of identity formation in some ways, and different in others. For each of these forms of self-alteration, pain lends the process meaning, while the final product gives credence to the abolition of an old self and creation of a new self.

3

Anorexia and Self-Mutilation
Diagnosed as Pathological

In several ways, modern-day eating disorder behaviors are manifestations of a quest for quasi-spiritual purity and transcendence. Like some religious ascetics and saints attempting to attain spiritual elevation, anorectics and bulimics inflict physical discomfort upon themselves to reach an ideal state of being that is obtained through the body, but has as its goal a state beyond material existence. Not only do they restrict their appetites and practice purging, they often mutilate their flesh.[1] Although sociocultural analysis is vital to understanding the near-epidemic appearance of eating disorders within the past three decades, the characterization of these disorders as self-infliction of pain has yet to be discussed. Starving oneself *hurts*. Consuming 15,000 calories in one sitting and then vomiting for an hour to purge oneself *hurts*. What does it mean when a human inflicts this kind of pain and discomfort upon herself?[2] To answer this question I will discuss anorexia as both an attempt to transcend the self by becoming pure and self-controlled and a simultaneous attempt to create an autonomous self. The implications of the relatively recent correlation of self-mutilation with eating disorders is important to the analysis of eating disorders as attempts to transform and initiate oneself into a new state.

As one of humanity's most common daily acts, eating provides sustenance, pleasure, social ritual, and social bonding. Eating is one of the most potent ways individuals interact with the environment as they incorporate physical elements outside themselves physically into themselves. Eating is one of our most basic and primal ways to manipulate the world around us in order to survive. We are fascinated with eating disorders because they refuse the exigency of nutrition and underscore the power of eating as a real and symbolic crossing of body boundaries. A

41

search for literature on eating disorders results in hundreds of references. Researchers have studied correlations between eating disorders and body image distortion, family conflicts, adolescent separation anxiety, conflicted sexual development, homosexuality, cultural pressure, obsessive-compulsive disorders, and plasma beta-endorphin levels, to name only a handful. Anorexia and bulimia are the two most commonly known eating disorders and have been labeled "modern diseases" due to the dramatic increase in their diagnoses in the past three decades.

Anorexia is also modern by virtue of its exclusivity to countries that are industrialized and have fairly affluent standards of living.[3] It was first diagnosed as a disease in the 1870s, a time of increasing industrialization, urbanization, and concern of the developing American middle class for maintaining civilized values against an onslaught of immigrants. In America, the association of food with spirituality, morality, and sexual identity dates back to Sylvester Graham's diatribes in the early 1800s against eating meat. Graham also preached against the vice of masturbation and claimed that eating meat increased carnal desire. Another early American health food missionary was John Kellogg, who in Victorian times presaged the current health food trend with his invention of granola.[4] Middle-class and affluent Victorians considered appetite a sign of sexuality and lack of self-restraint. Middle-class Victorian women felt pressured to uphold an idealized image of women as frail, morally and spiritually superior beings whose weak appetite and disdain for meat demonstrated purity and daintiness.[5]

Opposing the image of the ideal woman as one who languished in need of bedrest and water-cures, and epitomized temperance and bodiless spirituality, were women like Abba Woolson in the "woman movement." In 1873, the same year that the starving disease was labeled "anorexia nervosa," Woolson argued that women should develop their physical stamina to aid in their moral and intellectual development.[6] Perhaps the women who starved themselves were perversely exercising their physical stamina of self-denial. Or perhaps, caught in a cultural melange of contradictory options and messages, these women sought to create a well-defined identity for themselves. Cultural historian T.J. Jackson Lears characterizes the late nineteenth century as a time when "individual identities began to seem fragmented, diffuse, perhaps even unreal. A weightless culture of material comfort and spiritual blandness was breeding weightless persons who longed for intense experience to give some definition, some distinct outline and substance to their vaporous lives."[7]

Several "fasting girls" did experience what was probably the most noteworthy and attention-garnering experience of their lives by becoming weightless caricatures of the Victorian ideal of womanhood. "Fasting girls" not only captured the attention of their families but fascinated the public, and as late as 1910, the popular American press continued to report their cases. The public read about Sarah Jacobs, a Welsh girl known throughout Britain and the United States, who reportedly began to fast in 1867 and finally died of starvation in 1869. While many people, including Sarah Jacob's family, configured the emaciated girl as evidence of a miracle, doctors were skeptical. The rising prominence of medical authority and medicalization of the body that accompanied the Victorian hesitation between science and religion permitted the medical community to pathologize the anorectic body. Citing medical standards of expected bodily response to lack of food, doctors decried fasting girls as pathologically aberrant, or considered their prolonged fasting as fraud. The medical community considered Molly Fancher, a mystic and clairvoyant who was well known in the 1870s and 1880s and allegedly abstained from all but minute bits of food for fourteen years, hysterical, while Spiritualists believed she exemplified the existence of supernatural realms.[8] British physician Sir William Gull preferred to discard the imprecise diagnosis of hysteria and in 1873 described "anorexia nervosa" as a disorder of the central nervous system. Concurrently, French physician Charles Lasegue described *l'anorexie hysterique* as intimately connected to the dynamics and conflicts in the anorectic's family.[9]

Although she differentiates medieval fasting practices from modern eating disorders, Joan Jacobs Brumberg traces the history of anorexia and details the evolution of medical and psychiatric thought about anorexia in *Fasting Girls: The Emergence of Anorexia as a Modern Disease*. As a cultural history of anorexia, Brumberg's book is invaluable in understanding the contributions of Victorian norms and the ideas of Gull, Lasegue, Freud, and Pierre Janet to the modern perception of eating disorders. In the first half of the twentieth-century doctors continued to describe anorexia as a biological and psychological disturbance, to be treated with change of environment, forced feeding, and psychoanalysis. After World War II psychiatrists began to conceive of anorexia as a developmental issue, and theorists in later decades began to analyze anorexia as a reaction to cultural messages about the female body and gender roles. By 1988 the incidence of the diagnosis "anorexia" had increased to astounding proportions. Although within the general population eating disorders are relatively infrequent, and occur extremely rarely among African Americans, Chicanos, or many first or second generation ethnic groups,[10] the group at-risk for eating disorders shows a high incidence. In the at-risk population of white, educated, middle- or upper-class, adolescent girls, eating disorders may afflict from 5 to 20 percent of individuals. There has been a gross increase in the number of cases diagnosed since 1970.[11]

Eating disorders have recently been seen as a "me too" behavior, and a "group reaction,"[12] which exemplifies the poignancy of these disorders as a search for social identity. Individuals do not seek an isolated identity, but seek to establish themselves in relation to their culture. Recognizing eating disorders as social behaviors forces confrontation of questions central to this book. If enough people indulge in a behavior, is it no longer deviant? If an action is greeted by a small accepting community, is it mainstream or subcultural? What does the epidemic of eating disorders communicate about the culture in which it occurs?

Many works have been published in the past twenty years interpreting anorexia and bulimia as responses to cultural pressures on women. Factors that must be analyzed to understand eating disorders include historical and cultural attitudes toward the body, toward women, toward autonomy and the self, toward sexuality, and toward food. These approaches have been amply discussed elsewhere, and I will instead touch upon other, less acknowledged ideas, including a brief historical overview of attitudes about eating, eating disorders as masochistic behavior, and eating disorders as attempted self-transformation. An analysis of eating disorders will ultimately provide an avenue to explore the significance of other forms of self-mutilation.

The Quest for Spiritual and Moral Purity: From Piety to Pathology

It is well recognized that anorectic and other eating disorder behaviors are similar to ascetic and ritual religious devotions; however, the spiritual and psychological motives are often denied similarity.[13] In many cultures and religions devotees practice ascetic denial and mortification to enhance their spirituality, while sufferers of eating disorders present a complex array of motives. Eating disorders provide a launch point to discuss the nexus between self-inflicted pain and transcendence of the self, and self-mutilation as a vehicle for identity.

The quest for physical and spiritual health has often entailed dietary restrictions including fasting and ritualistic use of food. The Egyptians, for whom the body was spiritual terrain, practiced purging for three consecutive days each month to rid their bodies of food, which they believed was the cause of all sickness.[14] As long ago as 600 B.C. the Greeks connected regulation of the flow of blood outside the body with regulation of food in and out of the body. They encouraged an approach to curing disease that included bleeding to rid the body of bad humors that cause illness, starving to prevent the formation of new harmful humors, and purging the body to rid the body of any remaining debris.[15]

Accounts of medieval women who starved and tortured themselves in an effort to become saintly are presented in Rudolph Bell's *Holy Anorexia*. One of these women, Catherine Benincasa, not only refused to eat, but flagellated herself with an iron chain three times a day until blood covered her from shoulders to feet.[16] Although her family pleaded with her to stop, and the Church forbade her radical asceticism, Catherine continued to alternately fast and vomit any food she ingested. Eventually she even refused to drink water, and died shortly thereafter. Bell's case study of Catherine Benincasa connects secular psychological motivation and spiritual motivation, and furnishes early evidence of the connection between fasting and self-mutilation as ascetic behaviors. Bell contends that Benincasa's extreme behavior coincided with guilt over the deaths of two of her older sisters, for which Catherine felt responsible. In an effort to purge herself of her "sin," she turned away from worldly practices, became a religious zealot, and determined that she would conquer all exigencies of her physical existence. At the age of sixteen, Catherine sheared off her blonde hair and began her career in self-torture. She refused to speak for three years, deprived herself of sleep, and wore an iron chain bound tightly about her hips. Bell concludes from a minute examination of Catherine's life that her acts of strident self-control were attempts to atone for her guilt and render her autonomous from her familial bonds as well as her mortal existence. Her religious devotions rewarded her with visions that led her to believe she experienced mystical union with God. She was canonized as a saint by the Catholic Church and became a model for holy anorectics for the next two centuries.[17]

The holy anorectic who rejected the edicts of the Church, adopted extreme methods to declare her autonomy from family and sacerdotal authority, and become spiritually pristine, presaged the modern woman with an eating disorder. The holy anorectic rebelled against traditional rules and instead opted to become saintly by denying human desires and pangs of the flesh. Ironically, the saint's behavior was merely an extreme of officially approved behavior, just as the anorectic's thinness is a caricature of the ideal female body. Although extreme self-mortification was more accepted in medieval times than it is today, the motives for self-inflicted pain remain open to question. Although shifting from one cultural climate to another requires reinterpretation of behavior within its specific sociocultural context, the persistence of certain behaviors throughout time necessitates addressing the similarities as well as the differences.

Although psychologists often acknowledge the historical occurrence of religious masochistic behavior, few of them are willing to discuss spirituality or entertain the possibility that "deviant" behaviors may signal real or substitute religious experiences, or that myth, ritual, and spirituality may play a role in human physical and mental health and wholeness."[18] Religion is not ignored as a demographic factor, however, and research reveals the fascinating fact that Jewish and Catholic populations are at a greater risk than average to develop anorexia.[19] Likewise, although both modern eating disorders and religious asceticism have been placed in their cultural context, little attention has been given to the deeper psychological component of religious asceticism. Understanding medieval attempts to achieve holiness via fasting, vomiting, and self-flagellating provides insights into the modern preoccupation with similar behaviors in the secular sphere.

Eating disorders exhibit the same dialectic of simultaneous escape from and confirmation of self as other masochistic acts. Several psychologists conclude that bulimic behavior is an attempt to alleviate stress and tension, and blot out painful feelings,[20] thus recreating and consolidating the self by the physical act of purging. Anorectics also attempt to abolish an old self and create a new self, by actually threatening their own existence with starvation. The holy anorectics systematically challenged their ability to withstand pain and the disapproval of the church. On the one hand the holy anorectics were strong-willed mavericks, on the other they were conducting a crusade to abolish their own egos in order to experience communion with God as an ultimate spiritual union. Those who exhibit the same behaviors today struggle to become independent individuals within a secularized society that demands autonomy and material proof of success. The previous discussion of pain showed how it can facilitate self-creation and simultaneously function to heighten awareness of the self as witnessed by another. The asceticism that anorectics impose upon themselves is an act of reflexive sadomasochism, and illustrates the urgency of their desire for a connection with something beyond their own problematic individuality. They use their bodies as narcissistic self-objects to simultaneously escape and confirm the self through pain and the attention their actions accrue.

Analyses of anorexia and bulimia reiterate over and over the struggle for self-control and desire for a state of pureness. Anorectics exercise "supreme mind control"[21] in order to ignore the pain of constant hunger. Their self-imposed asceticism often combats a fear of losing control. Many anorectics fear that if they allow themselves to eat they will consume prodigious amounts. This in fact often happens, and anorectics then force themselves to vomit.[22] Anorectics seeks to master themselves through mastering the body. While some individuals may choose team sports to accomplish the same goal, anorectics, like those who pursue marathon running, body building, or martial arts training, choose the challenge of solitary discipline. As they separate the act of eating from previous patterns of social interaction and significance, anorectics become more and more absorbed with experiencing, and often publicly denying, their own physical and psychological experiences. They typically experience acute hunger and sensitivity to cold, noise, and fatigue, yet staunchly refuse to admit discomfort.[23] As the anorectic disassociates from the body she "appears to be insensitive to pain and fatigue; she acts like a fakir who is able to ignore pain."[24] Her self-starvation is an effort to prove her superiority over other people, and experience a feeling of pureness.[25] Many dieting women see abstinence from food as a statement "about virtue, empowerment, and cleanliness,"[26] and as a "form of absolution, of atoning for any digressions from [the] pursuit of a good body." This implies a disturbing preoccupation with the power of food consumption and body perception to determine self-worth for many women, not just sufferers of eating disorders. The anorectic carries the experience even further and imbues abstinence with the ability to confirm her ego and identity.

Religious attitudes proscribing indulgence in physical pleasures have often dictated ascetic attitudes toward food to confirm spiritual ego and identity. In *Summa Theologica* St. Thomas Aquinas stated, "Gluttony and lust are concerned with pleasures of touch in matters of food and sex."[27] Food consumption as a symbol of spiritual and moral degeneration in Christianity goes back as far as Eve eating the apple, although food regulations are certainly not solely a Christian tradition. In medieval culture, controlling the appetite, as long as it was sanctioned by the Church, was an accepted method of demonstrating the religious ideal of suffering and service to mankind. Fasting was considered "fundamental to the model of female holiness."[28] In the late 1500s Santorio Santorio, whose obsession with diet and weighing the body earns him the status of grandfather of the diet, explicitly equated the weighing of the body with the weighing of the soul.[29] Certain foods have been associated with witchery, concupiscence, and dissolution, and one need only peruse the Old Testament for examples of religious diet strictures. The medieval link between food and spirituality is only one example of the potential eating habits have to express what is most holy or most corrupt about human nature.[30]

Contemporary culture has revived the connection between health, food, and spirituality. The "mystical motif" of food symbolism has burgeoned in mass culture in the past three decades. New interest in the moral implications of vegetarianism, ecology, and an interest in Eastern philosophies has prompted an increased awareness about macrobiotics, the Yin and Yang properties of brown rice, and innumerable trends of food as medicine. In part a reaction against institutionalized medicine, the health food trend encourages people to self-define according to what they take into the body as nutrition.[31] Those who attempt to transcend former lifestyles and identities with strict diet regimes and symbolic behaviors are expressing a kind of magico-religious thinking in which certain food items or habits carry power far beyond that warranted by their known physical properties.

Anorexia is an example of magico-religious thinking that imbues control of the body with the power of establishing identity and self-worth. It has been noted that anorectics desire to conquer the body as the prime material of the self upon which they launch a battle of self-discipline and differentiation. Hilde Bruch describes the anorectic as appearing strong and vigorous, but internalizing deep feelings of ineffectiveness. Typically, an anorectic is the perfect daughter, acquiescent in every aspect of her life except her eating habits. In one small sphere the anorectic seeks to differentiate herself from her well-meaning, but often cloying and demanding parents, significant others, or stressful environment. As Bruch notes, "[S]ome feel that for the first time there is a core to their personality and that they are in touch with their feelings."[32] In the absence of other abilities to establish an independent identity, controlling food, which is a potent symbol of family life and connection, becomes a symbol of controlling interaction with family and others.[33] Combining a strange dialectic of submission to hunger, and exhibition of self-mastery, the anorectic embodies the control issues of both a dominator and a submissive.

Self-starvation becomes a pseudo-autonomy that is ultimately self-defeating. Maud Ellmann, who calls anorexia a "self-lacerating form of protest" against the pressures burdening modern women, notes that anorectics "collude in their oppression by relinquishing the perilous demands of freedom in favor of the cozy compensations of infantilism."[34] Although the anorectic resists familial or cultural control of her identity, she feels helpless to control anything except the narrow field of her body. This is true for adults as well as adolescents. As Kim Chernin discusses in *The Hungry Self*, "[T]he present epidemic of eating disorders must be understood as a profound developmental crisis in a generation of women still deeply confused, after decades of struggle for female liberation, about what it means to be a woman in the modern world."[35] One anorectic explained her self-destruction of her body by saying, "It was the only thing I owned, the only thing which could not be taken away from me."[36] The distressing contradiction of anorexia is that while it is an attempt at self-definition, it incurs the risk of self-annihilation. In an attempt to declare autonomy, the anorectic may die. The irony is that most anorectics don't want to die, they want to transform themselves by physical and metaphoric reconstruction of a new self. As the holy anorectic strove to achieve an enlightened state of being by resisting Church edicts against her unsanctioned starvation and driving her body to the exhaustion and debilitation that would induce spiritual visions, the anorectic fights both the cajoling of family members who see her thinness, and the persuasive cultural messages about standards of beauty for women that ensure she will always be conscious of being observed and evaluated. Faced with the dilemma of being incessantly visible and on stage, yet wanting to be visible as her own autonomous creation, the anorectic withdraws into a private belief system that equates self-worth and self-creation with mastery of her body. This self-recreation is also a motive of bulimic behavior.

Bulimia as a disorder is not clearly demarcated from anorexia because the two behaviors often overlap.[37] Many anorectics also exhibit bulimic behavior, often with the same intent of relieving psychological stress through body manipulation. Anorectics talk about the euphoria and feeling of pureness they experience from not eating, and bulimics, who vomit after ingesting large quantities of food, often refer to the calmness they feel after vomiting. Vomiting as an emotionally and physically cathartic behavior is not solely a medical, secular idea. Papago Indians vomit during rituals to induce rain to fall on the Sonoran Desert and some yoga practitioners train themselves to vomit at will. Vomiting ejects unwanted physical elements from the body and can provide emotional relief by symbolically purging the psyche of unwanted debris.[38] The bulimic "needs to cleanse herself, to deny the need for soothing, to throw up and out of herself what she cannot digest" either physically or emotionally.[39] Physical effects of vomiting include stimulated respiration and production of tears, which in turn relieve physical and emotional stress and induce a sense of well-being. In the aftermath of purging a bulimic temporarily feels sedated and calm.[40] She feels a brief sense of peace and is able to halt her food abuse temporarily. The act of self-induced vomiting produces feelings of mind-body integration and awareness of ability to control the body. The anorectic will ignore the pain of hunger by objectifying her body and disassociating from it. A bulimic will ignore feelings of satiety and compulsively eat until she is in pain, then use the trauma of regurgitation as a physically and emotionally integrative and cathartic experience. The purge is a simultaneous punishment for overeating and a redress of the problematic overfull stomach. In the redemptive act of purging, the bulimic clears her mind of guilt and fear of lack of control as she clears her body of unwanted food.

Both anorectic and bulimic behaviors are private rituals that challenge the body and use body sensation to combat feelings of alienation and distress and instill a feeling of calm. Because physiological events are concurrent with psychological events as previously discussed, the bulimic may feel temporarily healed. One of these reasons Western society considers this behavior aberrant instead of justified self-healing is that the practitioners are often unable to stop their behavior. In other climates, similar actions may be performed within a controlled, culturally sanctioned ritual, that provides a resolution that encourages the fasting or vomiting behavior to end.

The manipulation of the body to create altered states of being has many different connotations depending on context. Although sudden, unexpected physical sensations may cause mental flight, heightened sensory awareness may facilitate acute awareness of self and surroundings as unified in time and space.[41] The shock of a fall or sudden intense pain may cause loss of consciousness, while an extremely pleasurable sensation or prolonged endurance of discomfort may spark feelings of bliss and bonding. Runners describe the high they feel after a prolonged run. In the Yamana culture of Tierra del Fuego education of medicine men entails months of strict ascetic practice including long periods of motionlessness, tedious rubbing away of the top layer of skin, and extremely stringent dietary regimes. Holger Kalweit calls these practices "transpersonal psychotherapy" and "consciousness-raising techniques" that debilitate the body in order to free the mind of its daily habits and introduce a new and powerfully spiritual consciousness.[42] The difference between the reaction of mental flight versus acute awareness seems to be the intensity and duration of the pain. Sudden intense pain evokes an automatic response of the body that combats the pain with disassociation or loss of consciousness, whereas lower-level pain causes heightened awareness of the body. Bulimics experience the pain of overeating but then force themselves to vomit, thus inflicting more discomfort upon themselves, although purging ultimately provides relief. Vomiting may function as a self-inflicted mortification that reintegrates self with body and reinstates order.[43] This may be linked to the euphoric, integrating effects of higher levels of the natural opiate beta-endorphin that bulimics experience compared to individuals who do not habitually vomit.[44]

Purging provides a temporary feeling of self-control and ego confirmation. The vomiting phase of food abuse has one distinct advantage over the eating phase: it cannot go on indefinitely. It provides a momentary resolution to the consuming phase of food abuse, and leaves the sufferer temporarily exhausted. For a short time after vomiting, the bulimic feels back in touch with reality. One bulimic woman explains, "Breakfast I'd throw up. Lunch I'd throw up. Dinner I'd throw up. Afterward I'd think, 'Great I got rid of that bloated feeling,' and then I'd be able to refocus and do work, be productive. But a few hours later, I'd do it all over again."[45] The painful act of purging fulfills a function similar to the function of prayer as Brena describes it. Both instill a feeling of peace, enabling the devotee to conquer sensory experiences and concentrate on other responsibilities. As the devotee concentrates energy on her ritualized behavior, she rechannels her anxiety and establishes a sense of relation to *something*, whether it is expressed as communication with God or the food objects and sensations of her ritual. Although in reality sufferers of eating disorders have often lost rational control of their behavior, they are constructing a milieu of chosen actions meant to provide a familiar, safe haven and one way to feel effective and in control of themselves.

In many ways the struggle to master oneself is an effort to "come of age." Many psychological studies point out that individuals with eating disorders have difficulty negotiating the psychological boundaries between self and other.[46] This anxiety over autonomy often revolves around sexuality, gender roles, and the transition to mature adulthood that requires decisions about career and lifestyle. An individual in the throes of an eating disorder is desperately trying to become an individual, while simultaneously resisting adulthood and mature sexuality. Anorectics often speak of the contempt they have for their femininity and their desire to be androgenous. One anorectic testified to the pride she felt about her asexual body and her accomplishment in creating it. "Instead of growing up, I had as it were, grown down, and thus reversed a natural biological process. I was no longer a woman."[47] Another anorectic remarked, "I got my wish to be a third sex, both girl and boy."[48] Amenorrhea, cessation of the menses, is one factor used to diagnose anorexia. The anorectic who experiences amenorrhea symbolically loses her gender and becomes an entity that is neither man nor woman. Many anorectics are delighted with the physical and symbolic consequences of amenorrhea.[49] Chernin interprets shunning of menstruation as shunning what defines femaleness,[50] although this is perhaps too glib an elision of capacity to reproduce with gender roles. As anorectics resist their transformation into sexually mature women, they reject their gender "destiny," perceived as predigested and force-fed to them by society. Instead they attempt to self-design by imposing an androgenous ideal upon their bodies.

Eating disorders, like zealous religious practices of fasting, are often "an attempt to bring about either profound personal transformation or an entry into collective life and its spiritual meanings."[51] However, these goals are unattainable because the anorectic is not acting within a socially approved and structured milieu. In the attempt to void themselves of sexuality and hold physical maturity in abeyance, anorectics attempt to remain liminal; neither child nor adult and symbolically not human. The anorectic feels she is overcoming corporeal human desires and reaching a spiritual ideal of pureness, but is traveling a lonely road without spiritual guidance or structure beyond her own dietary rules and holy image of thinness conjured in her mind. She wishes to remain in an androgenous threshold state of presexuality. The anorectic, like the bulimic, never feels permanently recreated or at peace. She must continue her stringent diet to stave off the minatory approach of maturity.

Eating disorders become obsessive because they do not bring permanent psychic relief or confer recognized social status other than the attention of being considered deviant. Compulsive eating, purging, and starvation cannot fulfill the desire for individuation, pureness, and spirituality that the sufferers desire.[52] As Marion Woodman points out, "[T]he bread that becomes stone in the belly of the obese, the anoretic, and the bulimic is a cruel parody of the spiritual bread which they cannot assimilate."[53] The anorectic struggles to establish autonomy, but resists coming of age in socially conventional ways. She reaches for an illusory ideal that is an escape from the responsibilities and taint of the sexually mature adult who is fully assimilated into society. The anorectic's perceived pureness and individuality is a product of her attachment to her body as a narcissistic self-object rather than of a successful passage through a culturally determined and sanctioned initiation ritual. Perhaps this explains why so many anorectics and bulimics self-mutilate. Often sufferers of eating disorders scratch, cut, or burn themselves, or otherwise damage their bodies which have become the site of a fierce battle for identity.[54] The pain of self-mutilation may bring relief from the incessant tension and confirm the remaking of the body and self. Lacerating the body may function as a ersatz initiation rite and an attempt to force the self out of amorphous liminality.

Self-Mutilation as Self-Initiation

Apprentices who wish to become medicine men in the Yamana culture of Tierra del Fuego undergo a rigorous training process of stripping away their egos and previous thought patterns. Part of this process is a systematic excoriation of their skin. The apprentices rub their cheeks with wood shavings over a period of several weeks, gradually wearing away the top layers of skin until the exposed skin is painful to touch. As the outer layers are tediously removed, deeper layers of skin, endurance, and consciousness emerge. The apprentice has transformed his body and penetrated to inner regions of his soul by symbolically abolishing the barrier between his inner self and the cosmos as he diminished the skin barrier between external and internal body realms. Shamanic lore contains many examples of paranormal powers demonstrated by withstanding pain and physical injuries that miraculously heal without scars. These events acutely confirm the shaman's power to mediate between spiritual and earthly existence as he controls his response to pain and the mutilation of his body. The skin as the fundamental binding of people's physical being is one of the most basic mediums with which humanity interacts with the environment as they absorb information and are perceived by others. Mary Douglas's theory of the potency of body barriers as symbols of boundedness and protection also illuminates the significance of breaking the skin barrier. Although mutilating the body by penetrating the skin is in no way itself an act of mysticism or spirituality, the motivations and repercussions of the act reveal a great deal about the yearning to recreate the ego and transcend the conditions of existence.

Shamans benefit from their acts of self-mutilation because they live within cultures that valorize their acts. What do private acts of self-mutilation, unsanctioned and even condemned by Western society, accomplish? A teenage boy carves the word *hell* into his forearm and holds a burning cigarette to his skin. A woman in her early twenties locks herself in the bathroom after a fight with her boyfriend and makes incisions on her stomach and legs with a razor. A patient in a psychiatric hospital severely slashes her genitals. A young man who is bored and lonely shaves his head and tries to pierce his nipple with a needle. Acts of self-mutilation exist along a continuum ranging from those we label as signs of mental illness to behaviors we consider acceptable and even fashionable. The act of self-mutilation brings together the elements of body narcissism, ritualization, and pain in an attempt to resolve an identity crisis. Self-mutilation may take many forms and be motivated by many emotions and circumstances, but ultimately it is an attempt to carve a passage from one state of being to another by cutting, burning, or excoriating the skin. In one form, self-mutilation is an attempt to reintegrate the self from a fragmented state of depersonalization akin to the function of bulimic purging. On another level, it is an attempt to garner attention from, and reintegrate into, a social milieu from which the individual feels alienated.

Chapter 2 discussed sadomasochistic acts as interactions in which ritualized control and body sensation confirm self-perception and identity, and feelings of emotional connection to a partner, and sometimes invoke a spiritual experience. Similarly, self-mutilators, like anorectics and bulimics, are struggling with self-esteem and identity and are attempting to establish a feeling of connectedness. Although some psychologists see this process as an attempt to establish a previously nonexistent ego, Heinz Kohut sees the process as reestablishing a secure ego. He describes the process as an attempt to "bring about the lost merger (and thus repair the self)."[55] The pain of the body forces awareness of the wholeness of the physical self by sharpening awareness of body boundaries and limits. Discussing a self-mutilator, John Kafka explains that "problems of limits, the limits of her body, the limits of her power, and the limits of her capacity to feel—were of major importance in the analysis of [the] patient whose foremost symptom consisted of cutting herself and interfering with wound healing."[56]

The assessment of self-mutilation as an attempt to establish limits and overcome alienation from self and environment is supported by its correlation with eating disorders. It is also supported by the fact that skin-carving and other self-mutilatory acts are highly correlated with a history of incest and are described as part of a post-incest syndrome[57] in which an incest survivor copes with traumatized emotional and physical boundaries. A person who self-mutilates as part of post-incest syndrome may be demonstrating rejection of the past invasion of his or her body, and simultaneously making a painful declaration of the ability to control his or her own body boundaries.[58] As is the case with eating disorders, most of the individuals who self-mutilate are adolescent girls or young women. In a very simple way, self-mutilation, like self-starvation, is a plea to be witnessed and confirmed by others as proof of self-worth and autonomy. In the absence of the ability to perform structured, established healing rituals, the traumatized individual uses his or her body as primary material to self-heal. The individual symbolically and physically struggles to transform inner conflict into visible and feelable gestures. The act of self-mutilation often draws blood, symbolic of life and energy. As the blood crosses the broken skin barrier, the act of self-mutilation communicates pain and alienation. Self-mutilation is a powerful attempt to overcome distress, release inner tension, and enter a different state of consciousness. Individuals who self-mutilated as teenagers or young adults sometimes subsequently engage in sadomasochistic activity to achieve similar results.

An account of self-cutting poignantly demonstrates use of the body and pain as an avenue to express the unexpressable and relieve tension.

> Cutting began in the hot humid summer of 1987. Very drunk after a terrible fourth of July party at Laura's house. Within days of breaking up with Jeff, and really miserable about me, but blaming it all on Jeff and Laura and anyone else that would take the blame. Dying for some recognition or attention or just anyone to notice and prove that they cared about me, I took a razor from my desk drawer and moved it slowly across my wrist. Not much of a cut, kept trying to draw blood, and finally some came out of the intersection of three veins in my left wrist. I smeared some blood on a page in my journal so I could remember and add just a bit more drama to my already self-induced dramatic life. The next day after being at a Crosby, Stills & Nash concert with a lot of people who should have noticed the small but scabbed cut on my wrist, I went home and made the small cut deeper. This time I was really angry, and I cut hard with the razor into my already cut wrist. The sound of a bow being dragged across a violin string rivetted through my body. It hurt really bad. Then I walked around the house bleeding, unable to stop the blood from running down my arm, and still no one noticed. What about me? I couldn't get an answer from anyone. I decided no one cared. From here my alcoholism and drug addiction were my favorite ways to hurt myself and act out destructively. Not until five years later, three years into recovery and the date of my 27th birthday, did I feel the urge to cut myself again. I found the same razor in my desk drawer that I had saved over the years as a symbol of my pain. I made 27 small cuts on the back of my left hand, from the bottom knuckle of my thumb to the joint of my wrist. Someone at work noticed. I felt really dumb. I didn't cut again for about another 6 months. Now I am in a relationship and we are beginning to have really bad arguments, and

he says really hurtful things to me and then he leaves. I break a glass and cut the shit out of my right upper thigh, just slicing while I cry uncontrollably. Another fight, more cutting in the same spot. Another fight cut a pattern on my left shoulder, like where a tattoo would go. Another fight, a razor on the back of my left forearm. He gets very angry at me for cutting, and threatens to leave the relationship. I begin therapy and stop cutting for almost 9 months. Big big fight and I cut with broken glass my hip, so that it will be covered by underwear and unnoticed, because the rage needs to stop and I begin to hear voices in my head and it needs to come out and I feel so utterly crazy like I should be locked in a room for a long time and then I cut myself . . . and it all goes away. Relief. Another fight, same spot, and another fight, same spot. Sometimes you can see the scars depending on how tan I am at any given time. I haven't cut in maybe a month. I made a contract with my therapist not to cut. I have to call her before I cut myself. Feeling severely neglected as a child, the pain is very deep and very great, and I don't want to be overlooked or pushed aside any longer. Cutting seems to be a great self-destructive attempt to become human. To gain recognition, to prove to someone that I matter, and that I bleed too. In the course of my life, I have basically always opted for self destruction rather than projection of anger outward, it is much more comforting to implode rather than to explode.[59]

As acts of reflexive sadomasochism, self-starvation, bulimic purging, and self-mutilation are not true rituals, but are often ritualized. The anorectic will spend hours lingering over a single egg she has allotted herself or cutting a piece of meat into a specific number of pieces before allowing herself to consume it.[60] Bulimics will expend enormous energy planning binges and food abuse rituals and techniques.[61] Acts of self-harm are also often ritualized. The self-mutilator will prepare and cherish select items to perform her deeds and sometimes follow exact procedures for cutting herself and caring for the wound.[62] Because this ritualization is not communally supported,[63] these acts are void of sanctioned spiritual foundation, and are diagnosed as deviant.[64]

However, this does not deny that these self-mutilatory actions may be an attempt to achieve a feeling of connection akin to that provided by a cultural initiation rite. The ritualization of these actions points out the urgency of the need for structure and connection to something, even if it is to a razor or glass of tomato juice. Similar to the way in which the anorectic implodes her identity into her body and regulation of food intake, the cutter depends on her body and mutilating instruments as trusted self-objects that will bring her relief. Self-mutilators often describe their instruments of self-harm as objects of comfort and security.[65] The ritualization itself is motivated by a need to order chaotic feelings and feel reintegrated into a structured psychological and social system. The pain of cutting oneself replaces the pain of disorder and fragmentation, and provides momentary self-definition, as will be discussed more fully below. The self-mutilator invests the cutting instrument, the act of cutting, and the pain of cutting with the potency to bring her into being, similar to the power participants grant ritual and body sensation in sado-masochistic interactions.

An attempt to ritualize behavior and codify identity on the body by self-mutilation is a poignant attempt to externalize internal distress. During the talking cure of a therapy session, the client expresses feelings verbally. The client "gets it all out." In an act of self-mutilation gesture replaces language. What cannot be said in words becomes the language of blood and pain. Although the gestures are often performed clandestinely, they are potent expressions all the same. David Napier calls ritual a "primordial link to others,"[66] and the reconciliation of food abuse and self-mutilation as secretive acts and yet as attempted communication rests on their potential to be witnessed. Rarely do the end results of these furtive acts remain permanently hidden from the view of others. The anorectic exhibits her emotional struggle and protest with her physical appearance, which is public for all to observe.[67] Some anorectics enjoy displaying their thinness, as if the public attention their performance as hunger artists accrues nurtures them as food cannot.[68] Habitual purging, and scars and lacerations from self-mutilation cannot be hidden indefinitely from others. Although some self-mutilators proudly flaunt their wounds, others carefully hide them. This attests to the potency of the message they inscribe upon the body. For many self-mutilators revealing the origin of their scars is an act of vulnerability and a risky attempt to establish connection and trust with the confidant.

The shame of self-inflicted wounds expresses a dark side of the social context in which they occur. Kaplan examines the complexity of ritualistic behavior and of labeling a behavior "perverse."

> [I]f we remember that every human being is susceptible to
> the longings, anxieties, and mortifications that motivate the
> perverse strategy, the possibility that our everyday submis-
> sions to tweezer, facial scrubs, and the like are normalized
> variants of perversion should not offend us but alert us to
> something important about our shared human plight . . . [A]
> perversion, when it is successful, also preserves the social
> order, its institutions, the structures of family life, the mind
> itself from despair and fragmentation. For as horrifying as self-
> mutilation might be, the perverse strategy that empowers the
> behavior is aiming to prevent worse mayhem—homicide,
> black depression, utter madness.[69]

If we return to the Western preference for wholeness of the
body, what Bakhtin calls the classical body, which is self-contained and separated from profane connections with decay, death,
birth, or procreation, we understand the extent of the self-mutilator's transgression. Her "perverse strategy" is an act of making
her body "grotesque" in Bakhtin's term. Her body is no longer
smooth, and unmarred, but is a body in the act of transforming.[70]
Her blood shed connects her to the primal forces of life and death,
as well as to her ancestors and other humans. As she spills her
blood she is no longer separate from the external world but physically and emotionally spills out into it. By violating the Western
value of the classic body, the self-mutilator is staving off the more
extreme transgression of isolation, an emotional state of disassociation, and perhaps redirecting verbal or physical violence which
she consciously or unconsciously would like to direct toward
someone besides herself. In other cultural contexts this might be
considered a heroic act, or an act of passage to adulthood in
which one reconfigures oneself and one's actions as an adult. As a
private act of anguish, devoid of sanctioned cultural meaning, it is
diagnosed as pathological. If an individual feels unable to help
remake his or her world as part of a community, he or she
remakes the self.

Referring to "symbols that formally dissolve oppositions—
joints, the pineal body, the skin, autoimmunity," Napier asserts
that these physical elements "become the focus of a culture's
social and mental balance, a battleground on which its toughest
intellectual, moral, medical, and ethical issues are either com-
pounded or solved."[71] The proliferation of literature and diagnoses of eating disorders in the past three decades, and the recent

public awareness of self-mutilation proves Napier right. In 1985 the Phil Donahue Show aired a show on the topic of self-mutilation. The show received thousands of letters in response.[72] Since 1985 self-help groups and hospital programs have formed to combat the phenomenon of self-harm.[73] Public attention and fascination with body alteration, including masochistic and perilous acts, indicate a desire to analyze not just the neighbor's daughter who has dwindled to 82 pounds but American cultural identity as etched on the body. In spite of the proliferation of ways to self-define—perhaps because of the plurality of ways and lack of a cohesive communal structure for many individuals, the body has gained new importance as the ground upon which to stake one's identity. Faced with a multitude of choices and the exigency to declare oneself an autonomous outstanding individual, staking out the body as the primary territory for identity makes sense. As family and social milieus become precarious, individuals seek physical sensations of pain and pleasure to self-define and awaken an awareness of themselves as bounded individuals. The body remains a constant, controllable element with which to attempt communication and mastery of the self.

Self-Mutilation and Reintegration

Self-mutilation is "a complex behavior in which people deliberately alter or destroy their body tissue without conscious suicidal intent, or willingly allow others to alter or destroy their body tissue."[74] "Deviant" self-mutilation is "private, impulsive, [and] idiosyncratic."[75] Defining deviant acts is a difficult task, but a useful index is "the atmosphere of risk, secrecy and wrongdoing surrounding the behavior [as] a clue to the perverse nature of an activity."[76] This guideline points out the influence familial and social culture has on defining the normality of an action by teaching the individual to react to certain actions with shame or disgust.

Different types of self-mutilation were first explored by Karl Menninger in 1935 when he wrote about culturally sanctioned forms and pathological forms.[77] Most culturally sanctioned body alteration is performed during initiation rituals in which children or adolescents are demarcated as social and sexual beings, contingent on both the process of initiation and the final outcome of the ritual. An example is the male and female circumcision rituals in the Maasai culture. Although the significance is somewhat different for males than for females, the Maasai ritual mutilation marks the end of childhood and entry into the adult world for both sexes. Bearing the circumcision pain functions as a symbolic acceptance of the burdens of adulthood and rebirth into a new social role. A Maasai warrior explains, "You must put all the sins you have committed during childhood behind and embark as a new person with a different outlook on a new life."[78] Endurance of pain plays a significant role in imparting meaning to the ritual, as does the final body modification. The initiate passes through the liminal stage and emerges to reintegrate with society. Individuals may be attempting a similar journey with their "private" and "impulsive" actions.

Western society typically views body modification rituals as barbaric and defines similar actions by individuals as pathological.[79] As of 1988 the epidemiology of self-mutilation had been scantily studied, but several correlations with various personality disorders had been researched.[80] Prison populations often self-mutilate, while more than half of the self-mutilating population admits to having experienced symptoms of an eating disorder. The occurrence of self-mutilation in these specific populations points out the importance of social milieu when interpreting acts of self-mutilation.

Self-mutilation in the prison population is a unique phenomenon in which to explore the nexus between self-mutilation and environment. As an environment designed to place strictures upon the human body, prison is an environment Mary Douglas would concede is the epitome of control of physical expression. However, instead of inmates acquiescing to the prison system that attempts to maintain their physical existence at a survival level in which quietness, order, organization, efficiency, and tightly controlled time and space are the norm, inmates may rebel against their restrictions. Although some inmates may react by following the norms, other members of the control-oriented environment react by resorting to nonphysical "ethereal" expressions such as religion. Others subvert the control the system exerts over them in any way possible. One of these ways is to flaunt control over their body. A study of inmates shows that the one thing inmates feel they are able to control is their body.[81] Instead of quietly submitting to a structured regime in which they are told when to eat, sleep, and exercise, many inmates rebel and perpetuate a subordinate inmate culture. The dominant prison strictures remain as an umbrella environment, while the culture created by inmates is so powerful that many inmates feel it is inescapable.[82] Assimilating to the inmate subculture is a response to the extreme privation of inmate life, especially during long-term imprisonment. Inmates as single individuals in the prison institution have little power. They are placed in a dependent child-like position in which they can make few choices. Inmates are deprived of adult roles and sexuality and have little control over their interactions with other inmates or the outside world.[83] Although some prison environments have been constructed to be as domestic and comfortable as possible, most prisons are both understimulating because of lack of a variety of activities, and overstimulating because of inability to escape the presence of other inmates or of guards or to control the quality of interaction with them.[84] "Minutely controlled, stripped of autonomy, his self-image under severe attack, the inmate solves some of his problems through absorption of the inmate code. As the inmates move toward greater solidarity—so it is suggested—the pains of imprisonment become less severe."[85] Part of the inmate code is maintaining a façade of toughness and strength under any circumstances. Tersely explained by one inmate, "You have to perform" according to the inmate code of etiquette.[86] This is especially true of men in maximum security, long-term lockup but pertains to less restrictive incarceration and women's prisons as well.

In a circumvented way, prisoners often use self-mutilation to maintain a façade of toughness and status within the inmate subculture, while trying to cope with the larger prison environment. Self-mutilation by inmates is a complex action whose messages are unique to each individual and often unclear, even contradictory. Inmate self-injury is meaningful on many different levels: it may result from a failed suicide attempt or from untreated mental illness. It is often an adaptive strategy to gain personal, individualized attention within the prison. This interpretation of inmate self-mutilation implies that the inmate is trying to reintegrate into a social milieu that will provide him or her with recognition of his or her own humanity.

It is well recognized that acts of self-injury in prison are often attempts to obtain medical or psychological care.[87] An often verbalized reason for self-mutilating is the hope that the act will result in relocation to a different part of the prison. Inmates know that as a strategic ploy for attention, self-injury almost always works. "Less drastic moves are ignored and more drastic moves bring retribution."[88] In at least one instance, inmates self-mutilated as a group to call attention to their prison conditions. In

1971, 226 prisoners at the Kansas State Penitentiary in Lansing, Kansas, slashed their Achilles tendons in protest of a prison policy that they considered repressive.[89] In 1952 three dozen inmates "maimed themselves in a desperate attempt to attract public attention to the evils, the inhumanity, and the futility of the Louisiana penal system."[90] Self-mutilation in prison may result in redress. As the act of a lone inmate, it results in medical and sometimes psychological care. It may or may not be successful in winning attention for other desires, such as relocation. Explained as a cunning attempt to achieve a specific goal, it may or may not preserve an inmate's reputation as tough enough to cope with prison life.

Self-injury communicates more subtle messages that contradict the proclamation of imperviousness. Although inmates often claim that cutting or otherwise self-harming is a premeditated manipulation of prison staff and policies, it is often more than a conscious adaptive strategy. The act of self-injury in a routine and dull environment may indicate frustration and hostility induced by extreme boredom. Inmates often report that self-mutilation relieves tension, and many incidents of self-mutilation are performed while in solitary confinement. This echoes the motivations of self-mutilators who are not imprisoned and who also report physiological and emotional relief.[91] In an environment where the inmate is unable to freely express any emotion that may be construed as weakness, such as depression or sadness, self-mutilation may be a voiceless gesture of despair. In the prison environment where any sign of anger or outright rebellion will be punished, self-mutilation may signal repressed rage. Some inmates who self-mutilate report a satisfied feeling of revenge against the oppressive prison system when they obtain costly medical care and attention from staff.[92] One inmate's comment clearly shows that self-mutilation is a plea to be recognized and accepted as an individual rather than just another inmate. "I want to be noticed in here, you know, noticed as a person, and they [self-mutilators] want to be noticed as a person, so they break up their cell, and they say "Wow, look I'm alive, I'm a person. You see this? I cut myself, I'm bleeding, I have blood in me just like you."[93]

Self-mutilation is not limited to inmates serving long-term sentences. One study showed an 86 percent occurrence rate in the population of adolescent girls at a correctional facility.[94] A study conducted in 1991 of approximately 10,000 inmates, only 350 of whom were women, at minimum, medium, and maximum security facilities, showed that 3.9 percent of the men self-mutilated over a period of three and a half years, while only 2 percent of the women self-mutilated during this time. Interestingly, this ratio is a reverse of the ratio in the general population, noted previously, in which women who self-mutilate outnumber men who do 1.5 to 1.[95] In an environment where inmate culture provides the only cohesive daily community in a restrictive environment, self-mutilation seems to serve several functions. It reduces psychological and physical tension with a minimum of negative repercussions from prison staff and other inmates. It expresses emotions that are not otherwise able to be articulated. Most important, it necessitates response from prison staff that confirms the inmate's worth, and reminds the inmate that his or her flesh and blood are connected to the flesh and blood of all humanity. Like the self-mutilator who cuts to emerge from a state of disassociation, the inmate is using the body to reintegrate into the corpus of the human race.

4

Adornment:
Tattooing and Piercing

Written out on his body a complete theory of the heavens and earth, in his own proper person [Queequeg] was a wondrous work in one volume; but whose mysteries not even himself could read, though his own live heart beat against them; and these mysteries were therefore destined in the end to moulder away with the living parchment whereon they were inscribed, and so be unsolved to the last.

—Herman Melville[1]

Tattooing is not the hideous custom which it is called. It is not barbarous merely because the printing is skin-deep and unalterable.

—Henry David Thoreau[2]

Body mutilation has long been part of non-Christian cultures as a positive mark of identity, while in many modern Western cultures permanently marking the body has been considered degrading or deviant. Body modification practices are so prolific that an exhaustive account of the practices of body magic and marking around the globe is nearly impossible. Body mutilation such as scarring and tattooing often functions as part of a healing ritual, protection against forces that may cause injury, and admission to a social group. Cultural practices of body mutilation are often functionally akin to prayer as a practice that spiritually elevates an individual. The Syriac word *ethkashshaph*, for example means both "to cut oneself" and "to make a supplication." On the island of Tonga, people would cut off a finger as a sacrifice to the gods when a relative became sick, and many religions tell tales of self-mutilation and even self-castration.[3] As noted in chapter 3 in the section on self-mutilation as self-initiation, shamanic traditions often rely on body manipulation and subsequent altered states to propel the shaman into spiritual regions where he or she can develop shamanic abilities.

65

Several major religions exhibit complex attitudes toward self-mutilation and adornment. In the Old Testament, Leviticus 19.28 prohibits followers of Judaism from marking the body: "Ye shall not make any cuttings in your flesh for the dead, nor imprint any marks upon you." The Koran forbids marking the body. The Christian Bible associates body markings with sin as shown in the story of Cain, who was marked in punishment for slaying his brother. Christian traditions have supplanted autonomous practices of blood sacrifice with communal rituals, while using a brutal metaphor of self-mutilation to encourage purity. "If thy hand or thy foot offend thee cut them off and cast them from thee; it is better for thee to enter into life halt or maimed, rather than having two hands or two feet to be cast into the everlasting fire. And if thine eye offend thee pluck it out and cast it from thee" (Matthew 18.9). In the hierarchy of this metaphor, victory over the body serves the spirit, and physical destruction and disunity represent a sacrifice made to enter heaven rather than as a process whose value helps humanity obtain spiritual enlightenment. Theologically, Christianity opposes salvation through acts of individual will, although denominational and historical variations present a complex picture of the tension between asceticism and obeisance to church dogma. One way to interpret Jesus Christ's mission as Redeemer is that his death on the cross served as a sacrifice that offered all of humanity salvation. His crucifixion obviated the need for individuals to offer animals and grains to propitiate the gods and obtain salvation. In this Christian model of redemption through Christ, autonomous body modification or manipulation to appease God would be construed as heathen.

Still, many people apparently have continued to feel a need for confirmation of their religion by marking their bodies. The Judaic custom of circumcision persists. Coptic, Armenian, Abyssinian, Syrian, and Russian pilgrims returning from the Holy Land frequently acquired souvenir tattoos to commemorate their journey. At the turn of the nineteenth century, it was traditional for Gypsies to tattoo these pilgrims, and the tattoo marks became part of the pilgrim's social status. An example of this is the Armenian title for one who has made the pilgrimage which is *Mahdesi*, which translates as "I saw death." Because only religious pilgrims were tattooed, the religious tattoos were also known as *Mahdesi*. The tattoo is a code indicating a spiritual passage, or at least a religious pilgrimage. Similarly, in Turkey the souvenir tattoos were known by the Turkish word for one who has made the religious pilgrimage, *Haji*.[4]

These religious tattoos became symbols of entry into a higher plane of spiritual existence and exemplify the overlap between Christian beliefs and body magic. First documented by a traveler in 1660, common marks included dots in the shape of a cross at the base of the fingers and crosses on the back of the hand or inside of the wrist. Biblical scenes marked the bearer as a devout Christian, but also served magical purposes. Women chose Annunciation scenes to ensure fertility, and sufferers of illness placed tattoos on ailing parts of the body to promote healing. Although Greek and Latin Christian churches have criticized these practices, they persist, and many Muslim Arabs tattoo in disregard for the Islamic prohibition on marking the body.[5] Even today, many American tattooees have permanent religious icons and emblems as well as personal magical symbols inked upon their bodies.[6]

Body alteration seems to serve a need deeper than that addressed by modern Christianity or other institutionalized religious or cultural avenues in the Euro-Western world. Perhaps the oldest art known to human beings, and the most ancient method of expressing personal and communal spiritual beliefs, body alteration has persisted until the present day in various magico-religious and secular forms. Humanity seems unlikely to discontinue this very personal act of creativity simply because a religious authority decrees it unnecessary. Acts that simultaneously penetrate and alter the physical body, what Thevoz calls "self-retouching,"[7] connect people to the spiritual realm where spirit and body communicate and are intimately connected. Permanent body alteration in some cases has been ritualized into body adornment or masking as "self-substituting" efforts to construct identity, in which withdrawal into identity construction replaces socially structured forms of religious worship or spiritual value systems.[8] Personal meaning replaces, or at least supplements, cultural values. The spiritual meaning of body mutilation has been lost at times due to cultural and religious changes, and yet people incessantly and instinctively return to it as a means of expressing their deepest desires and fears.

Tattooing

Tattoos are prompted by "the primitive desire for an exaggerated exterior" and are manifestations of deep psychological motivations. They are "the recording of dreams,"[9] which simultaneously express an aspect of the self and recreate and mask the body. As products of inner yearnings, self-concepts, desires, and magical or spiritual beliefs, designs on the human body formed by inserting pigments under the skin have been crafted by nearly every culture around the world for thousands of years. Definitive evidence of tattooing dates to the Middle Kingdom period of Egypt, approximately 2000 B.C., but many scholars believe that Nubians brought the practice to Egypt much earlier. There was little anthropological attention to tattooing in the early part of the century because of preconceived notions of its insignificance to cultural analysis.[10] Archaeological evidence indicates that the Maya, Toltec, and Aztec cultures performed tattooing and scarification,[11] and that the practice is thousands of years old in Asian cultures.[12]

Although tattooing was practiced in pre-Christian Europe, the word *tattoo* does not appear in English until Captain John Cook imported it after a journey to the Pacific Islands in the eighteenth century. Captain Cook claimed the Tahitians used the word *tatua*, from *ta*, meaning "to strike or knock," for the marks they made upon their bodies. Captain Cook recorded this word as "tattaw."[13] The Polynesian word *tapu*, from which the word *taboo* derives, indicates the status of the person while being tattooed.[14] Although no connection has been made between the words *tattoo* and *taboo*, it seems highly likely that they are related. While enduring the process of acquiring socially meaningful marks, the tattooee is being formed and shaped into an acceptable member of society. Prior to the completion of the tattoos the person is not only physically vulnerable because of the possibility of contamination during the penetrating process of tattooing but symbolically vulnerable as well. No longer without a tattoo, but without a finished tattoo, the person's body and therefore the self are not yet completed. The person is a liminal entity not yet in society and therefore taboo.

Although the origin of tattooing is uncertain, anthropological research confirms that tattooing, as well as other body alterations and mutilations, is significant in the spiritual beliefs of many cultures. Various peoples tattoo or scarify during puberty rituals.[15] In traditional South Pacific Tonga society, only priests could tattoo others and tattoos were symbolic of full tribal status.[16] Eskimo women traditionally tattooed their faces and breasts and believed that acquiring sufficient tattoos guaranteed a happy afterlife.[17] In many African cultures scars indicate social status and desirability as a marriage partner. Scarification patterns often identify the bearer as a member of a specific village. Many of these practices are changing and fading as Western influences enter African cultures.[18]

Until the mid-nineteenth century, Cree Indians living on the Great Plains tattooed for luck, for beauty, and to protect their health. Cree men with special powers received tattoos to help them communicate with spirits. A dream conferred the privilege of receiving a tattoo, which would be inscribed during a ceremony conducted by a shaman authorized to tattoo. The tattooing instruments were kept in a special bundle passed on from shaman to shaman. The ability to withstand the painful and tedious process of tattooing, which often lasted two to three days, confirmed the tattooee's courage. Blood shed during the process was believed to possess magical power and was absorbed with a special cloth and kept for future use.[19]

In a Liberian initiation ceremony "the novices . . . are resuscitated to a new life, tattooed, and given a new name . . . they seem to have totally forgotten their past existence."[20] The ritual recreates the flesh bequeathed to initiates by their parents and experienced during childhood. The physical change marks a symbolic rebirth into a new spiritual, social, and physical reality as well as a real physical change. This magical use of the body reiterates the idea that physical and spiritual existence and their interactions are deeply entwined.

Marks of Deviance

European "civilizing" cultures often attempted to eradicate body marking practices, often in the name of religion. In 787 A.D. Pope Hadrian I decreed a ban on tattooing.[21] Constantine prohibited tattooing as an act of altering the body that God molded in His own image.[22] Puritans in the New England colonies connected body markings with witchcraft, and those suspected of practicing witchcraft were searched for "devil's marks" as proof of their alliance with Satan.[23] Quoting the Old Testament interdict against printing or cutting marks upon the flesh, the Puritans also condemned Native American tattooing.[24] By the 1850s many Native Americans had adopted the settlers' customs of dress and began to view tattooing as unnecessary and uncivilized.[25] Africans brought to the colonies as slaves often bore scarification marks of royalty,[26] social standing, or servitude,[27] which were probably perceived by the colonists as heathen tokens of savage cultures.

In some cultures, the elite class marks the bodies of individuals considered pariahs or marginal members of society. In the Near East, slavemasters sometimes tattooed slaves as a sign of degradation and branded incorrigible slaves. In late medieval and early modern Europe, slaveholders branded their slaves, a practice continued in France until the early 1800s, and in Russia until the mid-1800s. Runaway slaves in Brazil, the renegade *quilombos* who were branded if recaptured, considered their brands marks of honor and infamy.[28] In Yoruba, where body markings placed one within society, slaveowners denied their slaves distinguishing marks of social status. Exemplifying a much different assumption about body marking, slaveholders in the Americas branded and tattooed their slaves to place them firmly outside mainstream society. During the eighteenth century, prisoners incarcerated in France were physically marked.[29] The use of body markings as positive signs of identification and inclusion in many African societies contrasts sharply with European use of the marks as signs of degradation and marginalization.

The American association of tattooing with exoticism solidified in 1851 when Dan Rice hired a tattooed man named James F. O'Connell to appear in his circus.[30] During this time Rice was also fascinating America with another body image in popular culture, the blacked-up minstrel. The minstrel representation of the black body was replete with complex meanings of manhood, race, and class.[31] The tattooed body on display was probably less familiar but equally intriguing. Without evidence of what kind of tattoos Rice's employee had, or whether or not he performed, or served only as a display object, it is difficult to assess the meaning of his existence. Perhaps O'Connell conjured images of a white savage, halfway between the articulate, civilized white man and the Native American who expressed his culture with paint and body markings. Perhaps audiences saw the tattooed man as Melville's Queequeg incarnate; exotic, half-blackened with ink—and half-black, but not without feeling or humanness. P.T. Barnum followed Rice's success by displaying an elaborately inscribed Albanian named Constantine, who was an extremely popular attraction. Barnum was the first to exhibit a tattooed woman, in 1898, which added the erotic element of viewing the female body.

During the latter part of the nineteenth century as the public became more familiar with the art of tattooing through the circus, which was primarily a working- and lower-class entertainment, tattoo was also developing commercially. The first known professional tattooist in the United States was Martin Hildebrand who who had an itinerant practice during the Civil War and opened a shop in New York City in the 1890s.[32]

At the turn of the century, tattoos showed up in titillating and disreputable places. Tattooing became a shop-front industry in the disreputable Chatham Square area of New York City. Electric tattoo machines made tattooing cheaper and less painful, and good tattoos easier to render. With this new technology, tattooing became popular among the lower classes and quickly came to be associated with blue-collar workers and ruffians. Although tattooing was an upper-class trend for a brief period, by the 1920s the middle class considered it deviant. Tattoos were considered "a decorative cultural product dispensed by largely unskilled and unhygienic practitioners from dingy shops in urban slums," and consumers were "seen as being drawn from marginal, rootless, and dangerously unconventional social groups."[33]

In the 1930s, the American fascination with body alteration as a deviant practice continued. During this time a psychiatrist and writer named Albert Parry often wrote about the significance of tattoos and embedded stereotypes of deviance in the public discourse. Although Parry was an avid fan of tattooing, and bemoaned its decline in popularity,[34] he called tattooing a "tragic miscarriage of narcissism."[35] He claimed tattooing was a substitute for sexual pleasure, evidence of homosexuality, and a source of masochistic pleasure.[36]

Parry associated tattooing with deviant sexuality. Although the exhibition of a tattooed woman in the circus in prior decades was tinged with a hint of sexual voyeurism, Parry explicitly constructed images of tattooed women as abnormal and accessible commodities. He claimed that five percent of American women were tattooed and insinuated that beneath their conventional clothes, these disguised women had marked their bodies with signs of desire and erotic adventure.[37] Parry stated that "prostitutes in America, as elsewhere, get tattooed because of certain strong masochistic-exhibitionist drives." Parry reasoned that prostitutes obtained tattoos because they desired yet another reason to pity themselves and were seeking to be mistreated by clients. He also asserted that they believed tattoos would prevent disease and that they obtained sexual pleasure from the tattoo process. As proof of the prostitute's urge to self-humiliate, Parry described several tattoos of cynical humor and sexual innuendo inscribed upon prostitutes, such as "pay as you enter." Conflating racism, homophobia, and the idea of women as a sexual commodity, Parry also claimed that English prostitutes etched names of their pimps on themselves or likenesses of "their Negro lovers, much to the chagrin of American sailors," while French women inscribed the names of their lesbian lovers, and gay men tattooed themselves in order to seduce young boys.[38] Parry relished the stereotype of tattooing as a perverse and deviant activity. His assertions reverberated for decades in the assumptions psychologists held about tattooed man and women.

Tacitly based on the preconception that marking the body is deviant, psychologists have sought to determine a connection between tattoos and psychopathology. Members and potential members of the military who bear tattoos have served as subjects for several studies that correlate tattoos and social adjustment. A study in 1943 concluded that "psychopathology or social or emotional maladjustment is significantly higher among tattooed than among nontattooed men."[39] A 1968 study concluded that sailors with tattoos were more likely to be maladjusted, and military men with "Death Before Dishonor" tattoos were more likely than nontattoed sailors to be discharged from the service.[40] Other studies conducted during the late 1960s link tattooed women with homosexuality and masochism and tattooing practices in institutions with high levels of aggression, sexual insecurity, and social maladjustment.[41] These studies both preselected the subject pools and ignored the effects of the institutional milieu on the tattooees.

Other studies of imprisoned populations reveal motivations to tattoo that are similar to the motivations to self-mutilate as a reaction to the surrounding environment. Similar to inmate self-mutilation, tattooing may provide relief from the numbness of incarceration and establish individual or gang identity.[42] A 1964 survey of the public perception of tattooed persons revealed that a majority of people perceived tattooed individuals as physically strong and psychologically aggressive. This survey concluded that whether or not tattoos are indicators of social maladjustment, they may function to enhance the bearer's self-image and integrity.[43] Returning to the theory of confirmation of the self in a pain-enduring sadomasochistic interaction, one can understand the connotation of toughness and integrity that a tattoo confers. One psychoanalytic case study observed that a dominatrix in a sadomasochistic relationship bore her tattoos as evidence of her ability to manage the ritual infliction of pain adroitly.[44] This self-mastery and "toughness" earned her the right to control her submissive partners and proved her ability to alter both her own and her partners' consciousness and identity.

Meaning: From Deviant to Mainstream

The lack of understanding of the functional purposes of both the tattooing process and the final marks have led to a perception of tattooing as barbaric, deviant, and sexually perverse. Dominant American culture has considered tattoos as marks of degradation, criminality, and marginality. Without an understanding of manipulation of the body to inspire "sacred awe" in viewers and bearers of tattoos and other body alterations, one can not grasp the significance of these alterations as tangible establishment of personal, spiritual, and social identity.

Although body modifications such as tattooing and piercing have been construed as signs of deviance, during the past two decades body alteration has begun to filter into mainstream culture as a popular form of self-expression. Articles about tattooing and piercing proliferate in popular literature. Fashion magazines show models with tattooed ankles and pierced navels, and recruit well-known tattooed musicians for their pages. Children are able to play with tattooed dolls.[45] Exhibits of tattoo art are shown in art galleries.[46] Piercing boutiques and tattoo shops are conducting brisk business.

Several factors have encouraged a "tattoo renaissance" since the 1950s.[47] Post war prosperity along the West Coast combined with a new interest in Asian cultures, many of which revere tattooing. The Japanese, for instance, have a long tradition of tattoo as an intricate body art.[48] New technology and interest in tattooing as a fine art have produced new aesthetic standards, a wider clientele, and an infinite variety of tattoo designs, including "neo-tribal" stylistic forms that are heavily influenced by tattoo traditions of other cultures. Today, as sociologist Clinton Sanders notes, tattooing has become more professional and more of a fine art. Tattoo artists are much more likely to have formal artistic and academic training than in previous years and to consider their tattooing practice a creative pursuit. A more diverse population is getting tattooed in the past two decades. New tattoo clients are better educated, have more disposable income, and care more about the decorative and aesthetic elements. Customers often custom design their own tattoos and the tattooer-customer relationship is changing from one of service provider and buyer to a collaborative effort.[49] The relationship between a piercer and his or her client may be even more intricate and personal. With or without conscious realization of the significance of body making in other cultures, Americans today are adopting similar practices. To understand these practices as cultural phenomena, we must first understand their significance for individuals.

The Significance of Pain

Tattooing and piercing are not just adornments added to the body surface like jewelry or cosmetics—they penetrate the flesh. Piercing is a quick process followed by several weeks of tenderness while healing. Tattooing is a tedious, painful process followed by a period of transformation in which the wound heals and the redesigned body emerges. These adornments, like self-starvation and self-cutting, accrue significance from both the process of physical transformation and the final product. The tattoo procedure is often a "highly social act"[50] in which an individual manipulates and asserts identity within a specific social milieu. Getting a tattoo is often "a social event experienced with close associates," who provide moral support, offer advice, and help pass the "anxiety-filled waiting time."[51] Many tattoo artists and piercers comment on the large percentage of their customers who belong to college fraternities or sororities and get pierced as part of the initiation process. It is rare that these individuals tattoo or pierce alone. Often several associates accompany the initiate to provide companionship and fortification.

Many cultures attach social status to body alterations and consider pain a crucial element for imparting meaning to body alteration. Yoruban scarification is not only considered aesthetically pleasing but announces the marked individual's fortitude and ability to endure pain. A Yoruban woman acquires her markings when she is old enough to marry and accept the painful ordeal of childbirth. Her *kolo* cicatrices "exhibit her willingness to bear pain. . . . Aesthetic value is bound up with the value of endurance and the willingness to bear discomfort to accomplish a greater good."[52] Tiv women remark on the ability of scarification to indicate masculinity and the desire to withstand pain in order to be attractive: "What girl would look at a man if his scars had not cost him pain?"[53]

Withstanding the pain of tattooing and other body alterations is also significant in American culture. The tattooee or piercee, like any initiate, vulnerably awaits the pain and new status the procedure will impart. Enduring pain is often considered crucial to gender constructions and demonstration of toughness. Although some tattooees have a difficult time bearing the pain,[54] others see it as a "good pain."[55] Part of the pleasure of a tattoo is the macho implication of being able to bear the pain, and during the 1950s and 1960s getting a tattoo was a common rite of passage into adulthood for many young men.[56] Still today, withstanding the tedious and painful process with bravado may be required to gain membership in a youth gang, or to demonstrate rebellion against authority.[57] College fraternities may require members to get tattooed or pierced as a sign of their loyalty.[58]

One tattoo artist with many tattoos connects the pain of the process with the pleasure of creativity. "It's a strange metaphor to say that pain is like an orgasm—but it is in a way. And it's like labor too . . . to go through this pain to create a thing, to get it out of you. The design is inside of you, it just wants to get out."[59] The creative expression of identity is enhanced by the feeling of "aliveness" that accompanies the pain of the process for many people. "This sense of existing, of feeling, of enjoying life, [comes] to many with the touch of the needle."[60] The prolonged pain produces euphoria for many,[61] and pain is also a meaningful and enjoyable element of the piercing process for some piercees as well as people who indulge in body branding or scarification.[62]

Marks of Transition and Status

Individuals who tattoo and pierce imbue the body with narcissistic or magico-religious powers to confirm identity and connect them to either a deeper self-awareness, a social group, or a vision of integration with the cosmos. Similar to the way in which the self-mutilator or anorectic physically demarcates a change in self-awareness and interaction with the surrounding milieu, an individual who chooses to self-mark physically confirms a change in status.[63] The "badge of admission" may carry personal meaning as well as a message of affiliation with a religion, one other person, a community, a youth gang, a fraternity, a military organization, or any specific group. The complexity of the action lies in the fact that the confirmation of identity is based on distancing the self from a large nonmarked portion of the population. Body markings are marks of disaffiliation with the mainstream and "visually proclaim a sense of camaraderie to others so marked."[64]

The change in status, similar to the self-mutilator's change in tension level and temporary "cure" of feelings of fragmentation,

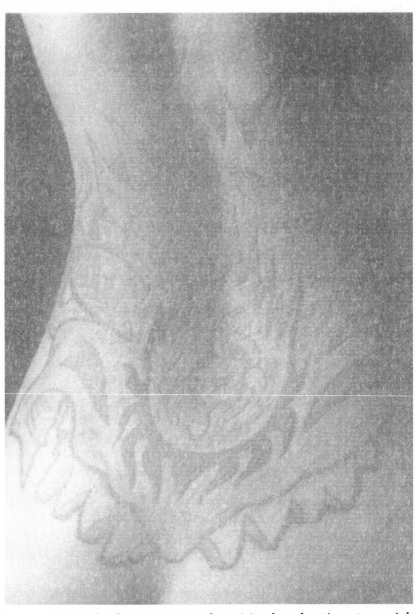

Fig. 1. A tattoo that began as part of a spiritual exploration at age eighteen. The tattooee calls it "The Knowledge Plant" and keeps adding to it through the years. (R., personal interview, March 22, 1996.) (Photo: John Davis)

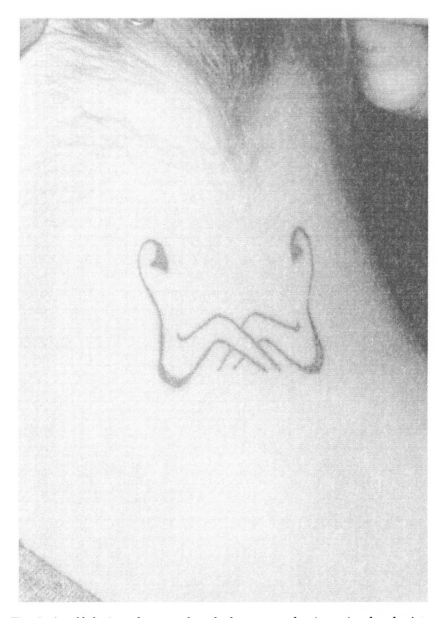

Fig. 2. A self-designed tattoo that declares sexual orientation by depicting two stylized women facing each other. (Sarah, personal interview, March 9, 1996.) (Photo: John Davis)

sometimes signifies an attempt to overcome a distressing experience and alter self-concept. Other times, especially with tattooing, the experience is more of an aesthetic than an emotional transformation. Tangible transformation sometimes approaches a mystical experience (Fig. 1). Approximating Thevoz's theory of the ability of masks to induce "sacred awe," one piercee commented, "I enjoyed the mysterious separation from the everyday." Another noted, "I think my [piercing] jewelry magically transforms a piece of flesh into a work of art."[65] Marking the body is a form of self-definition, and may symbolize lifestyle decisions about career choice or sexual orientation (Fig. 2).[66]

Body alteration and adornment are often used by women to mark a life transition and often conveys erotic appeal, marital status, genealogical background, and self-expression. Although only recently popular in America, body modification has long served these purposes in many other cultures. Moroccan women use henna to mark their hands and feet with elaborate designs as part of a marriage ritual. Although the markings fade within weeks they serve as both public announcement of the woman's change in social status and private codification of a life change. Deborah Kapchan describes the long henna process as one that "pivots the bride into the private realm of her own thoughts and sensibilities"[67] as she prepares for a life-changing event.

The physical change is also spiritual. The henna is said to contain *baraka*, a "divine blessing," that "works through the physical body to effect the metaphysical one."[68] The henna marks are physical, spiritual, private, and social evidence of a new status. The hennaed woman also fasts, which enhances her ritualized process of physical, spiritual, and social transformation. In contrast to henna ceremonies that prepare a Moroccan woman for marriage, "secular" or non-marriage related henna ceremonies are self-initiated. These events emphasize self-expression and "signify sexual self-possession rather than initiation." The decorative designs establish the bearer's claim to her own body.[69]

Self-Stigmatization
Body alteration functions in similar ways in Western culture, but it accrues a different potency as a deliberate choice of identification because of the stigma it incurs as a rebellion against, rather than an embodiment of, dominant cultural values. American women, fully aware of the stigma attached to tattooing and body alteration that doesn't help achieve standard beauty goals for

women, are more likely than men to choose adornment that is not publically visible and attach more personal meanings to their markings. In a culture that has taught them to preserve their bodies for the enjoyment of others, women who tattoo themselves are implicitly making a declaration of independence from at least some aesthetic standards expected of them by families, friends, and society. One 21-year-old woman explained the reaction of her mother to her tattoo. "She asks me to keep it covered if we go out in public. It is a sign of disrespect to her."[70] One woman explained, "I did this not for my husband, not for my parents, not for a boss, not for anyone else but me . . . my internal reason was to make a statement."[71] Women mark their bodies as an act of reclamation of their identity after a divorce, as a gesture of healing from sexual or other physical abuse, or simply as self-celebration. Body alteration symbolizes "control over and pride in the physical self" for many women.[72] Centuries ago, this tangible evidence of self-control and self-celebration may have been enough to convict a woman of witchcraft and sentence her to death. If a "devil's mark" was found on the body of a woman accused of witchcraft —whether self-imposed or organic in reality—it was interpreted as a chosen mark that confirmed the woman's autonomous nature and rebellion against prescribed behavior. Her willful desecration of her God-given body proved her collusion with the Devil.[73] Today, a woman's self-creation carries less formidable consequences. Similar to the ways in which punk styles of "leather and metal access forbidden gender symbols and behavior," for women,[74] tattoos and piercings provide a form of gender rebellion. Taylor's 1970 study highlighted this idea when one of the woman subjects proclaimed her motivation to tattoo as "I want to act like a boy . . . anything they can do I can do better."[75] Tattooing and body piercing blur previous assumptions about gender roles for both women and men.

Historically considered a salacious and pagan badge by Western cultures, deliberate body alteration proclaims defiance of cultural standards for both men and women, and many body modifiers enjoy the shock value of their adornment[76] and take pride in their stigmatized identities. Piercers and tattooees reject mainstream norms of adornment while simultaneously embracing subterranean status. This is an especially important component of the body modification trend for adolescents who are trying to establish social identity and autonomy from parental authority. The decision to tattoo or pierce signals an attempt at rebirth in which the adolescents choose to become autonomous. Recreating the body differentiates one from one's previous childhood body, and conventional familial and cultural milieus.

One connection between body alteration and youth and popular culture is explained by Daryl "Bear" Belmares, who had been a professional piercer for nine years in 1996 (Fig. 3 and 4). Belmares attributes the rise in piercing popularity since 1990 to the influence of media and describes two general motivations to pierce. Some people are entranced by the trendiness of the look. "They come in and say 'I saw it on MTV.' They've seen the Aerosmith video that has a model with a pierced navel and think it looks sexy." Their main motivation is a desire to be different. These individuals are likely to let their piercing heal over after a few years. Other piercers are "functional piercers" who spend more time premeditating their decision and pierce for sexual enhancement, to consciously mark a transition in their life, or to heal emotional scars. Although one might think that women are more likely to pierce as a narcissistic use of the body to establish identity, based on the proportion of self-starvers and self-cutters who are women, Belmares denied this gender distinction, noting that his clientele is 50 percent men and 50 percent women.

However, according to Belmares, women are more likely to pierce for therapeutic reasons.[77] One scenario in which a woman pierces to heal an emotional wound might go as follows. A woman who has been sexually abused feels alienated from her body and sexuality. She does not feel in control of her past or her sexual expression; she feels like a victim. She is numb sexually, both physically and emotionally. This woman may choose a genital pierce to recreate and reclaim her body. If she is conscious of her motives then her choice to undergo a painful moment and a healing period is especially empowering. Even if she is not fully aware of her motives to pierce, she benefits from the process of integrating her psyche and body through an ornamental pierce. She may choose a piercing that enhances erotic sensations and cannot help but become aware of her body sensations as her body heals. During the healing period of several weeks she must wash her piercing twice a day, lavishing care on a part of her body and psyche that had previously been injured. As the woman's body heals, so does her sexual psyche. The woman has relinquished the role of victim to choose an identity that includes adornment and eroticization of her body. Her act of self-creation coincides with a realization that she can control many aspects of her sexuality,

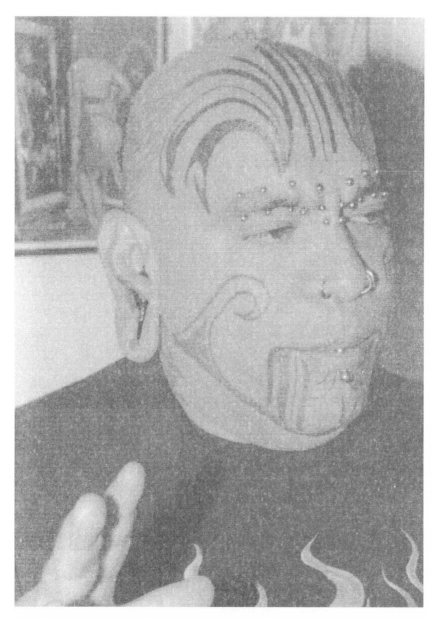

Fig. 3. Daryl "Bear" Belmares discussing the spiritual dimension of piercing. He began adorning his body on his eighteenth birthday and has multiple tattoos and pierces, and has cut his earlobes to insert ornamental plugs. (Daryl "Bear" Belmares, personal interview, March 9, 1996.) (Photo: John Davis)

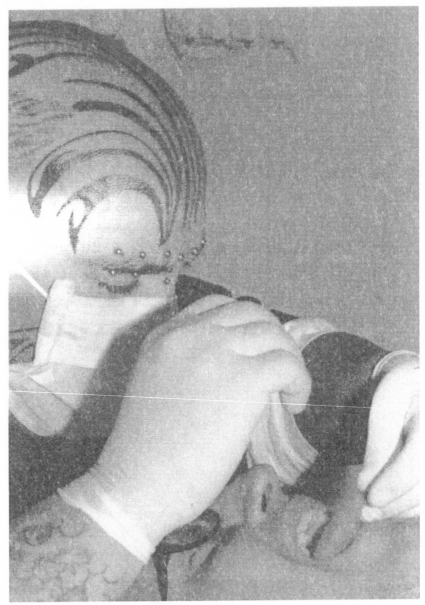

Fig. 4. Daryl "Bear" Belmares preparing to pierce a client's tongue. Here he is preparing to mark the site of the pierce. He will immobilize the tongue with forceps to pierce it. The whole procedure takes about ten minutes, the actual piercing takes an instant. (Photo: John Davis)

body, and identity. What was once numbed and detached, physically and psychologically, begins to feel alive again.

The body-art renaissance has sparked a sophisticated use of body alteration as a source of identity and adornment during the past three decades, although the general public continues to see these practices as deviant or at least unusual, especially if an individual shows interest beyond "acceptable" decoration, that is, a single tattoo or pierce.[78] The association with deviance and unconventionality empowers body alteration to be "primarily a mechanism for demonstrating one's disaffection from the mainstream. Tattooing [and] body piercing . . . are employed to proclaim publicly one's special attachment to deviant groups, certain activities, self-concepts, or primary associates."[79] However, as body art becomes more popular, its relevance as a mark of unconventionality will change. One wonders whether the body art trend, which is already accruing many advocates and attention in the mainstream media, will be able to sustain its romance with marginalization, or whether it will soon become a mundane act of conformity. Already, pierced navels or single rose tattoos on a woman's ankle have lost the ability to shock.

Although it is tempting to reduce tattoos to ornamental patterns imposed on the blank surface of the skin that are expressions only of personal identity, past and current practices refute this simplistic interpretation. The message of a public tattoo is not only its content but its existence as a display of public identity. Symbols of identity that are used to construct identity in the eyes of others carry meanings far beyond their physical existence. "Self-symbolizing" as Peter Gollwitzer calls this self-construction and presentation, is based on the desire for an audience to witness the act of identity construction. Gollwitzer points out that individuals are more likely to self-symbolize during times of identity-related anxiety.[80] This supports the interpretation of body alteration as confirming self-initiated identity and lends a clue to the proliferation of body art in our contemporary culture in which individuals constantly seek new avenues to declare their autonomy and uniqueness. Whereas once tattoos were considered marks of degradation, now individuals take pride in their self-stigmatization and publicly display colorful and elaborate tattoos. The difference between publicly visible and private identity marks is the degree of witnessing desired by the tattooee or piercee. This dynamic of self-construction that requires the observing power of a witness echoes the dynamics of narcissistic and sadomasochistic interactions that require recognition by another to confirm identity. Tattoos and other symbols of identity may reassure the bearer of an otherwise tenuous self-concept or reinforce an existing self-image. By completing a process of identity construction with a physical body change, one reduces the anxiety of liminality. Rather than having a community inflict marks of initiation, a self-marked person determines his or her own self-construction.

This self-construction is intimately tied to social perception. Regardless of the tattoo design, which may be a military insignia, a heart with a name, a tribal design, or any of an infinite number of unique and personally meaningful symbols, the tattoo is a declaration of uniqueness. Some people may have symbols, names or likenesses of heroes, relatives, lovers, or alter egos. Magical symbols, cartoon characters, family insignias, nicknames, faces of loved ones, or erotic pictures may be etched upon the skin. Others may have custom designed patterns or scenes. As permanent and public displays these body adornments simultaneously individualize the bearer and affiliate him or her with other body modifiers.

Although public perception is changing, as will be discussed below, a visible body mark is still symbolic of rejection of mainstream culture and its ethic of appropriate image and control of the body. In contrast to religious creeds that dictate reverence for God's finished work of the unmarred human body, body alteration glorifies the human body as unfinished, to be adorned and recreated. Only gradually is it becoming accepted as adornment and as a sign of self-proclaimed identity.

Piercing

The trajectory of piercing from an underground activity to a fashion in mainstream magazines illustrates the American adoption of marginalization as a trendy practice. Piercing various parts of the body, which is a more or less painful procedure depending on the body part, has become more popular and commercialized in the past two decades, and extremely fashionable in the past few years.[81] Although some people self-pierce, most individuals go to a boutique that pierces and sells piercing jewelry. Clients frequently request nipple, navel, and nose piercings, and less commonly obtain eyebrow, lip, cheek, or tongue piercings. Piercings through various glans or skin folds of the genitals are even less common.[82]

Although one can construct histories of self-mutilatory beautification practices, such as leg-shaving, hair-tweezing, and body sculpting, body piercing practices in Western cultures remain virtually undocumented. James Myers, an anthropologist at the University of California remarks on the stigma attached to body piercing and discussion of Western "nonmainstream" body mutilation, and notes that the general public conceives of people who pierce, scar, brand, and burn themselves as "psychological misfits."[83] Myers refutes any connection between these practices of body modification and pathological self-mutilation, and he discusses body modification as a cultural rite of passage. Although Myers attempts to normalize the perception of body modification, his ethnographic research is problematic because it is conducted with a select group of participants, a greater than average proportion of whom are gay and involved in sadomasochistic activities, therefore already marginalized by society. A more representative sample of the general population might show that certain forms of piercing have now become popular in mainstream culture, whereas the more extreme pierces have gained popularity with individuals who engage in what dominant culture defines as deviant.

Nose and navel piercings have become more common in the general population. It is probable that until now few individuals pierced ornamentally, and those who did rigorously hid their unusual adornments from sight. Ear piercing, once considered barbaric for women and a badge of homosexuality for men, is now an accepted, common practice for women, and has lost much of its stigma for men also. Punk subculture introduced multiple ear piercings to the public eye, and fashion spreads quickly popularized the look with a large percent of the population. The marginalized groups that contributed to popularizing ear piercing, homosexuals and youth subculture, are also responsible for introducing other body piercings into the public arena. As of 1993 a well-known and burgeoning piercing Los Angeles boutique, the Gauntlet, which originally catered to a large gay population when it opened in 1975, performed 18,000 piercings a year.[84]

Piercing practices have been pathologized as expressing sexual perversity and affiliation with marginal members of society, and as with tattooing, it is difficult to separate myth from reality. Tattooing has most often been mythologized as a proof of masculine heterosexuality, but the association of tattooing with gay culture has some validity, as tattooist Samuel Steward, also known as Phil Sparrow, notes. In his diary accounts of his years as a tattooist, which he kept for Alfred Kinsey's research at the

Institute for Sex Research, Steward estimates that fewer than 1 percent of his clients were obvious homosexuals and perhaps a total of 20 percent were gay. Although Steward acknowledges that his customers sometimes exhibited homoerotic motivations,[85] masochistic pleasure, and even fetishistic tendencies toward tattooing their own bodies or others', his experiences as a tattoo artist in Chicago in the 1950s led him to conclude that the homosexuals he knew were reluctant to tattoo because they considered it marring the body unaesthetically. Psychiatrist John Money is one of the few contemporary psychiatrists to discuss tattoos and body alteration, although he only discusses them in relation to pathology. He analyzes tattoos as possible indications of sexual preference and as an allurative display designed to attract certain kinds of partners. Money also discusses extreme forms of self-mutilation that are not decorative. The cases of self-castration he analyzes are often related to gender rather than sexual orientation. Because they are often desperate attempts to transform when other medical avenues have been exhausted, and are neither decorative, nor oriented toward a change in consciousness I will leave them to be discussed elsewhere.[86]

In contrast to the association of tattooing with heterosexuality (no matter what its homoerotic undertone), piercing is typically associated with male homosexuality, perhaps because of its prior acceptance as a feminine form of self-adornment and the connotation of jewelry and fashion as women's domains. Steward dates a change in men's attitudes toward fashion in 1954, when the *The Wild One*, starring Marlon Brando as a leather-jacketed outlaw was released. As an iconic moment for gay men, the movie provided a spark for the gay leather movement and a more pronounced desire for style and swagger in mainstream culture. Steward reports that there was no immediate increase in the number of his customers eager to acquire a permanent emblem of identity etched on their skin, but by the mid-1960s there was a definite gay minority involved in the sadomasochistic scene, who began to pierce their bodies.[87] These hypotheses are difficult to confirm, as are estimates that 10 percent of the population are tattooed or pierced.[88] A 1985 survey conducted by *Piercing Fans International Quarterly* determined that 52 percent of their subscribers were gay or bisexual and that 57 percent engaged in "dominant-submissive play,"[89] although by virtue of their subscribing to a journal about piercing this group is probably not representative of the general population.

Piercee demographics have changed in the past twenty years, and continue to change. Punks and heavy metal music musicians began to pierce in the late 1970s, and by 1990 the clientele of the Gauntlet included Axl Rose and Nikki Six of the heavy metal bands Guns n' Roses and Motley Crue, respectively, who came to get their nipples pierced. Another piercing shop opened in San Francisco where "tattooed counterculturalists" of all kinds came to get pierced noses, nipples, navels, and tongues, as well as even more exotic piercings.[90] Today, "for rebelling adolescents, piercing is the ultimate Mohawk."[91] However, adolescents aren't the majority of piercers. Demographics have shifted, and currently the typical piercing client is a middle-class adult described as "normal,"[92] meaning a heterosexual who does not indulge in sadomasochistic practices. "Bear" Belmares provides more precise description of the piercing population and its shifts in the past few years. In 1994, Belmares estimated that 60 percent of his male customers were gay, as were 20 percent of his female customers. Although he caters to clients of all ages, most of them were between 25 and 35 years of age and at least 40 percent were Caucasian, with Hispanic individuals comprising the next largest percentage.[93] Belmares claimed that only a small percentage of his clients explored sadomasochism.[94]

Two years later, Belmares's clientele had shifted. In 1996, Belmares described his piercing clients as "running 50/50" in its ratio of male/female, and gay/straight, and about half of his clients were involved with sadomasochism.[95] Belmares noted that his reputation, and the aesthetic of piercing had spread in the tight-knit community involved in sadomasochism. His observation about demographics may also reflect a fresh willingness of his clients to confess nonstandard sexual orientations, or perhaps a new willingness in society to experiment with nonstandard sex play. As part of our culture's fascination with marginality, individuals seem to respond strongly, albeit not always openly, to anything that connotes perversity, especially fetishistic use of the body.

In the meantime, Belmares also noted an increased use of piercing for therapeutic purposes. Many of his clients may not be fully conscious of their motivations to mark their bodies, but others are painfully aware. Most piercing sites are at points that allow physical passage between the external world and the internal body and facilitate interaction between the individual and the world through sensory input and expression. People choose piercings on their tongues and lips, on their eyebrows, noses, ears, and genitals. Most interesting is a navel pierce, which occurs at the site of the umbilical cord from which every human received prenatal sustenance. Many cultures consider these areas potent sites for physical and spiritual contamination; adornment of these sites almost seems to be an attempt to magically protect them or draw energy to them for strength or reinforcement. In other cultures similar actions might be construed as attempts to open the body site and its corresponding sensory and mental perceptions for spiritual enhancement, or to close the site to negative spiritual energy. Like Yoruba *Egungun* costumes that allow spirit possession to occur, or special masks that frighten away bad spirits, a piercing may consciously or unconsciously be imbued by the piercer with the ability to channel his or her energy or heal past wounds. Many individuals, especially women, come seeking resolution of past emotional, sexual, and physical abuse. Although every individual chooses a piercing for a unique reason, some therapeutic piercings are more common than others. Many women who have suffered sexual abuse choose genital piercings.[96] Research on the sites at which individuals repeatedly cut themselves might show that self-mutilators also mutilate certain parts of their body for specific reasons related to physical or emotional trauma that is connected to that body site.

Unlike piercers who pierce solely for the look, functional piercers often value the process of transforming their bodies as well as the product. Instead of one pierce, they return periodically to further adorn their bodies, and often enlarge their pierce by using larger and heavier piercing jewelry. Often they build a relationship with the piercer, who comes to know them and may take on the role of confidant, almost akin to therapist or medicine man. After getting his tongue pierced by Belmares, one client proclaimed, "He is my psychic father." Belmares had helped the client transform his "God-given" or "parent-given" body, not only fathering the new body of his client, but aiding his client in fathering his own body. Previously, Belmares had suggested the same client get a brand on his body, and advised the Chinese character for enlightenment. The client stated he had been more at ease since the brand. He had "needed it," he said, and had felt its effects.[97] There was an obvious affection between the piercer and his client, and the piercing episode illustrated that part of the potency of body alteration may come from the relationship between piercer and client. The piercer fulfills a role similar to the role of shaman in other cultures, as he advises and helps heal his clients through body alteration and helps his clients make their dreams and desires tangible. As the piercer changes the client's body, the body responds with surprise, releasing endorphins and engendering a mood change as well as a mark upon the body. As the piercee experiences the language of the body, he or she may be aware of an emotional change. Although the procedure may be painful, if a piercee cries it may not be so much from the physical pain as it is part of an integrated mind/ body reaction to the healing of a past trauma.

Sometimes piercees may use body modification to cope with trauma or stress present at the moment. Vanessa Alvarez (Fig. 5), a professional piercer for six years also distinguishes between individuals who pierce for the look and those who pierce for more significant reasons. She places herself in the latter category and explained her many tattoos and pierces by describing them in part as a coping reaction to stress similar to the coping mechanism of cutting. "Some people cut, I pierce." A crucial difference between self-cutting and piercing is the planned and ornamental nature of piercing. Each of Alvarez's tattoos and pierces has a unique meaning, but several are extremely personal memorials that speak about events in her life. As a professional piercer and brander, she has seen a variety of clients who pierce and brand for a variety of reasons. The popularity of piercing in recent years has brought into her shop many college-age men and women who typically get navel or tongue piercings. Alvarez noted that before piercing became trendy, her clients were more interested in less visible pierces, and were motivated by the erotic value of genital piercings, the transformative value of body art, and body modification as part of a sadomasochistic aesthetic.[98] The popularity of piercing suggests that although it has become a spiritual venue for some, for others it has become a fad. The difference is often marked by an attitude like Alvarez's. Piercing and tattooing are part of her everyday life and one of her coping mechanisms for transforming stress or traumatic events into tangible, contained messages upon her body. As she modifies her body, she controls some aspect of the event or her emotions. Her use of body art is a form of modern day body magic.

Piercing as part of a transformation, therapeutic process, commemoration, or celebration is ritualized more frequently than ever before. Clients want the piercing performed in their home as part of a ceremony that includes friends and family. Sometimes

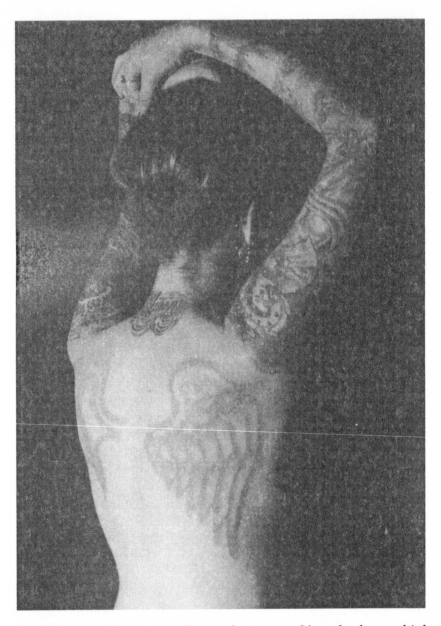

Fig. 5. Vanessa Alvarez, a professional piercer and brander, has multiple tattoos and pierces. The right side of her body is adorned with images of the Virgin Mary and other symbols that express her religiosity. She dedicated the left side of her body to the idea of sin and her "dark side" and adorned it with less holy images. Note the inscription "amen" at the base of her neck, while (not shown) she had the word "lust" tattooed above her pubic area. At age 25, she decided to get wings branded onto

they want it photographed like any other special event that marks an important life change. The piercees imbue not just the final pierce but the process with significance, and want it witnessed.[99] Perhaps piercing is nothing more than a New Age fad, a fanciful avenue for psychic healing and holistic health that Americans have striven for since the days when Sylvester Graham lauded bread as a spiritual substance. However, as Huxley pointed out, the urge to attain "self-conscious selfhood" is a universal wish, and piercing fulfills that urge for some people. Whether it is considered fetishizing the body as a narcissistic object or achieving wholeness of selfhood through pain and body transformation, piercing is gaining popularity.

James Myers describes the participants in his research on body alteration as "remarkedly conventional sane individuals. Informed, educated, and employed in good jobs, they are functional and successful by social standards."[100] He notes various motives for piercing, including sexual enhancement, enjoyment of the pain and pain as part of an initiation ritual, aesthetic enjoyment, affiliation with specific groups of people, "religious/ mystic" reasons, and enjoyment of the shocked reactions of others.[101] His final conclusion is that "[f]or the purpose of affiliation with a desired social order, people surrender to what is dearest to every human being: the body itself. When viewed this way, modification of the surface of the body is more than a visible badge of admission; it is also a primary connector of one's psyche to one's social group."[102]

As in the tattooing procedure, pain is sometimes an important element of piercing. Although many individuals pierce only for aesthetic reasons, they too have to endure the pain of the piercing and healing period. Piercing is often an ordeal to be stoically accepted in order to recreate the self and perhaps gain admission to a specific chosen subculture. Although some people may glean erotic pleasure from the pain of piercing, others are extremely apprehensive. Most resign themselves to it as part of

---

her back because she had "always wanted wings." The right side is an angel's wing, the left side, a devil's wing. The procedure took 40 minutes with a laser and has not completely healed in this picture. Alvarez described it as the worst pain she had ever felt in her life—a combination of being burned and electrocuted that made her nauseous. Surviving the branding experience assured her that she could bear the pain of childbirth. (Vanessa Alvarez, personal interview, April 17, 1996.) (Photo: John Davis)

the process.[103] Unlike self-mutilatory acts of cutting or burning one's flesh, piercing is not usually an attempt to emerge from an emotionally distressed state or gain relief from unbearable immediate tension. However, the piercee is seeking to transform the self and may be using the body alteration to resolve emotional trauma. Myers's research suggests that many piercees are conscious of a need for a rite of passage that is "painful, bloody, and mark producing" and recognize their appropriation of ritual elements of other cultures. As Myers notes, "The recognition of a need for an initiatory experience is one reason why the term 'modern primitive' is so popular with many contemporary American body modifiers."[104]

Body modification is a reflection of the contemporary impulse to react to what Kauffman calls "the numbing effects of hyper-industrialized life by treating the cultures of the world as one big spiritual supermarket."[105] Although Myers does not include extensive quotes that address the spiritual reasons to pierce, various interviews in tattoo and piercing trade journals support the idea that many people use body adornment as a narcissistic endowment of their bodies with magico-religious powers. As they modify their bodies they recognize the integration of body and spirit. In an interview in *Skin & Ink*, a tattooist who is both tattooed and pierced explains the meaning of her body alterations as they relate to her spiritual development. Many of her tattoos are spiritual symbols and she calls her body modifications a "mini-magical support system."[106] Although many tattoos are of Christian icons, many express a non-Christian spirituality that reflects various Native American and other religious beliefs. Tattoos and piercing jewelry often incorporate Celtic, Maori, and custom-made designs.[107]

For many piercees "piercing is a spiritual outlet in a society that long ago lost its taste for dramatic rites of passage." One piercee says that "other people internalize their rituals, we put them on our body. They're little celebrations of life." Some couples for example, get matching piercings to confirm private marriage vows. New uses of the human body to transcend material existence indicate that as one magazine article declared "the human body just isn't what it used to be."[108]

Mainstream Fashion

Interest in self-mutilation has expanded beyond anthropological study of other cultures. Performance artists and punks introduced self-inflicted wounds as decorative and deliberate means of communication. Their use of body modification to convey messages about society prompted a reevaluation of the practices formerly considered pathological. Anthropologists and psychologists are beginning to reanalyze the significance of ritualized self-mutilation. Art critics are beginning to contextualize tattooing within the history of Western art. Body modification is becoming an exalted art form and topic of popular and scholarly discussion, as specialized publications and articles in mainstream media discussing body alteration proliferate.[109]

The moment that body modification irrevocably entered the public eye was 1993 when supermodel Christy Turlington sauntered down the fashion runway with a navel ring. Although Zandra Rhodes, who designed punk-influenced fashions in the 1970s calls piercing "anti-fashion," Paul Gaultier's 1993 Paris show drew body modification firmly into the fashion pages. Gaultier acknowledges the origins of his inspiration as the underground club scene, sadomasochism and fetishism, the gay community, punk influence, and spirituality expressed with the body. Several well-known models, including Naomi Campbell, have pierced their navels and several have tattooed. As a fashion statement, the body and body alteration have become "more important than clothes."[110] Ironically, as body modification becomes fashionable and trendy, it loses significance as a personal choice and garners importance as a cultural fad that will peak and then pass. In 1992 the Food and Drug Administration approved a new laser technique that makes tattoo removal easy, and the decision to tattoo less ominous.[111] The commodification process has stripped piercing of its significance as a painful initiation as fake piercing jewelry has entered the market, and even bubble-gum machines sell fake tattoos. One can masquerade as a brave self-stigmatized subculturalist, while shirking the pain and permanence of real body alteration.[112] However, the painful process and permanence of the product remains an integral part of the significance of body modification.

At the turn of the century when the United Stated was experiencing the inchoate pangs of mass production, consumer culture, and creation of the self through image, Thorstein Veblen theorized that clothing fulfills a "spiritual need" by indicating social status and standards of taste and decency via conspicuous consumption. Body ornamentation fulfills the same purposes, as well as several others.[113] Because these adornments are products of a painful process and tedious healing, they qualify as bodily mortifications that Huxley claimed may lead to blissful and visionary experiences that impart knowledge and self-awareness. Without inflicting severe pain, they "surprise the body"[114] and most likely induce a chemical change in the brain that affects mood. Body modification has become popular as a modern therapy to achieve a "manipulatable sense of well-being."[115] As an expression of self-marginalization and affiliation with nonmainstream culture, body modification is an effort parallel to other forms of self-mutilation. Like an anorectic, bulimic, or self-mutilator, the tattooed or pierced individual is attempting to rip himself from the homogenous mass of people and establish an ego that communicates effectively with the environment. A stigmatized, emaciated, abraded, or tattooed identity is better than a fragmented ego, and perhaps more attractive than other alternatives our society offers.

5

Edging toward the Mainstream

A society that no longer puts on carnivals and costumed events loses an important psychological resource and impoverishes the collective imagination.

—Ginette Paris[1]

No masks can belong to us definitively or exclusively; masks belong to the divinities. They are symbols through which we communicate with the multiplicity of archetypal reality. As soon as we begin to get acquainted with the interior presences, we need a psychology that does not strive to eliminate the secondary personalities in order to reinforce the monologue of the ego.

—Ginette Paris[2]

During the summer of 1994 I witnessed a window display in the student section of Montreal with a theatricality unlike any I had ever seen before, except maybe in the red light district in Amsterdam. I had wandered into a shop selling various biker and leather paraphernalia, and as I left the shop I joined a small crowd gathered gazing into the display window. I edged into position to obtain a view of a young woman having a tattoo etched upon her body. I was initially stunned by the lack of privacy for what seemed like such an intimate transaction. Ironically, my second reaction was annoyance that I had been separated and held at bay from that intimacy, like the rest of the street spectators, by the window glass. As a marketing strategy to create desire, the live demonstration in the shop was brilliant. As a member of the audience I was able to gaze into the window, but unable to participate unless I, too, decided to get tattooed. Then I could obtain not only the same body art commodity as the woman in the window but the same attention. In exchange for my Canadian dollars and a few hours of pain, I, too, could become a work of art and perhaps provoke envy and desire.

One of the contexts in which to understand the increasing interest in the body as a canvas upon which to express one's self is the birth of performance art in the 1960s. Although humans have manipulated the body and its image throughout history, performance art as a reaction against the commercialization of art offered an accessible alternative to high art or high fashion as a means to express one's spirituality, politics, humor, sexuality, and creativity. The triad of the sexual revolution, civil rights, and youth culture in the 1960s introduced new attitudes toward the body and its realities of both pleasure and discomfort and laid a groundwork upon which today's awareness of the interrelation between corporeal existence and mental health has been built. As art movements and youth culture of the 1950s and 1960s incorporated aspects of the sexual revolution and the influence of black culture, attitudes toward the body gradually evolved from previous standards of social propriety. Discussion and exploration of sexuality, the effects of drugs on the body and consciousness, and self-representation through expressive clothing and adornment began to filter into mainstream media in the 1970s. During the 1960s and 1970s performance artists responded to and contributed to the reification of self-expression through the body.

Although body art of the 1960s was not solely a woman's art or a feminist statement, proud declaration of the female body and women's experiences has been a seminal motivation for performance artists. Performance art as an expression of feminist ideology often fought the standardized, contained female body as part of the rebellion against prescribed gender roles. Feminist art, like much performance art, presented women's insides. Judy Chicago's 1971 painting entitled "Red Flag," which depicted a close-up view of a woman removing a tampon blatantly exposed the reality of menstruation. The presentation of an image that would have been unthinkable a few years earlier, and the presentation of it as a work of art, violated cultural taboos about the body and art. The graphic depiction of menstruation speaks, and makes visual, the previously unspeakable and unshowable. Because of the potency of menstrual blood as an inner fluid that enables life, the image is a powerful claim for women's importance to the human race. By depicting a process in which what is inner flows out of the body, the painting metaphorically confirms the potency of women's perceptions and inner life. The image reminds the viewer that these realities will not vanish, no matter how securely some individuals tuck them away, how unpleasant some people may consider them, or what cultural taboos prohibit speaking of them.

Lynda Nead acutely notes, "If the tradition of the female nude emphasizes the exterior of the body and the completion of its surfaces, then women's body art reveals the interior, the terrifying secret that is hidden within this idealized exterior."[3] Carolee Schneemann's performance of "Interior Scroll" in which she extracted a poetic text from her vagina, vividly illustrates the attempt women were making to reify their artistic and biological potential. Schneemann's performance symbolically placed the poetic text on par with woman's capability to reproduce, and proclaimed the womb the source of creativity. By portraying body functions graphically, body art not only refuses to whitewash, standardize, or repress the human body, it also challenges ideas of artistic propriety by crossing body boundaries and revealing the inner workings of the human body. Performance works that crossed body boundaries entailed eating, vomiting, and self-mutilation. Other crucial works used the artist's body to blur gender boundaries, and play with representations of masculinity, femininity, and androgyny. While accepting the physical realities of the body as artistic media, many performance works pointed out the cultural construction of the body, sexual desire, and gender roles. Many artists have continued this tradition. Two of the better-known performance artists are Annie Sprinkle and Karen Finley, who have gained reputations for their willingness to publicly violate the culturally encoded standards of the female body. Annie Sprinkle exposes assumptions about the female body in several ways as she routinely masturbates on stage and invites audience members to look into her cervix as part of her performance. Karen Finley undresses matter-of-factly on stage and coats her body with raw egg and glitter, parodying the process of making the female body delectable, consumable, and desirable, and repudiating the cultural standard of classical sanitized beauty.[4]

Another sphere in which crossing physical and symbolic boundaries assumed importance during the 1960s was race relations. While attempts to legislate civil rights alternately succeeded or failed, American popular culture was incorporating African-American culture. In *Greenwich Village 1963: Avant-Garde Performance and the Effervescent Body*, Sally Banes points out the importance of African-American culture and discourse about race to the arts, especially arts during the 1960s that used or depicted the body. Although Banes states that American culture was assuming a "radically" Africanized component in the early 1960s, the African-American influence on dance and music had long been strong, if unacknowledged, in the United States. Similar to the Beat poets of the 1950s who sidled up to black culture with anticipation and admiration, artists of the 1960s who sought new expressive techniques often turned toward black language and gesture. By recognizing interest in the black body as an extension of modernism, Banes recognizes it as a "essentialist positive primitivism" that allowed crucial exploration of physicality. The avant-garde of the early 1960s not only integrated performance crews on stage and in film but purposefully crossed social and racial barriers by turning away from the standardized, "etherealized" body and styles of Euro-American culture and turning toward African-American influenced aesthetics.[5] The avant-garde performance valued gesture over language, randomness over predictability, the experience over a tangible product, and audience participation over separate arenas for performers and audience members. The contribution of African-American aesthetics to these elements spurred the vanguard of the 1960s forward, with results lingering well into the 1990s.

A smaller, much less acknowledged influence on the avant-garde scene and the augmenting physicality of the arts is homoeroticism. *Gay culture* is an ambiguous term to define, let alone trace, as are the problematic terms *gay sensibility* or *gay community*, but an aesthetic that addresses homosexuality, either directly or by insinuation, forces reevaluation of the physical interaction between individuals and social codes of conduct that restrict expression of sexuality and the physical self. The importance of the body and the cultural molding of its behavior to gay ideology existed prior to self-conscious gay ideology. One could start with Walt Whitman's poetic celebration of the body and its sensual pleasures, which caused an uproar in the 1850s. Whitman proclaimed "I am the poet of the Body and I am the poet of the Soul" in *Song of Myself* and embraced existence in the physical world as imbued with spiritual meaning. "If anything is sacred the human body is sacred" proclaimed Whitman in *I Sing the Body Electric* as he catalogued the wonders of male and female bodies from tongue to armpit to toe joints and concluded that "these are not the parts and poems of the body only, but of the soul."[6] As Allen Ginsberg followed this tradition in the 1950s, artists began to address the homosexual body in literature. The specific influence of a small segment of gay culture in the 1970s on fashion and the popularity of body piercing will be discussed later in this chapter, while one example of how homoeroticism has brought manipulation of the body into the art world will suffice here.

In the 1970s and 1980s the photos of Robert Mapplethorpe forced viewers to confront gender construction, homosexuality, sadomasochism, and the relation of pain and pleasure to sexuality. Mapplethorpe's 1982 photos of champion bodybuilder Lisa Lyons raise questions of gender construction as she poses in shots emphasizing her muscular biceps and taut thighs, while also displaying her breasts and pubic hair. In one particular photo Mapplethorpe photographs Lyons with a femme hat. The hat veil demurely covers her face, while she reveals her bulging hard bicep in an ironic display of the female body. If the picture were viewed in a magazine of typical pornography or a book of conventional erotic art, the viewer might have expected a passive female displayed only for the viewer's pleasure. Instead the viewer gazes upon an object of desire who is also a self-constructed and physically powerful female—characteristics typically considered masculine reframed as feminine and sexy. A 1980 portrait entitled "Smutty" depicts a young bare-chested man gazing coyly at the camera. The combination of his androgynous, allurative come-on and tattooed arms configures the youth as a stereotypical homoerotic image that combines the biological male with seductiveness that is conventionally considered feminine. Self-portraits of Mapplethorpe in 1980 show him in makeup that is usually worn by women, emphasizing an androgynous presentation and forcing the viewer to question his or her own standards of beauty and gender definition.

Other photos present more difficult dilemmas. Mapplethorpe's glossy high fashion presentation glamorized sadomasochist leather and metal wear in several 1978 photos of people bound, penetrated, and engaged in various homosexual acts. Several photos show a penis laced to a board in various phases of mutilation. Although these images are polished and carefully composed, their content is brutally graphic. By portraying sadomasochism as a work of art, Mapplethorpe turns what would be considered pornography in another context into a new form of performance art between consenting adults. The photos ask the viewer to consider the aesthetic value of physical mutilation of the body as art, pleasure, and self-expression. While Mapplethorpe's photographs speak only as the product of one artist and certainly are not representative of homosexual desires, through homoeroticism they reintroduced the body to the viewer and forcefully questioned the way in which it was to be witnessed.[7]

The shifting attitude toward the body has culminated in claims for the body as a medium for political statements, and as spiritual territory as well. Holistic New Age philosophy dictates a union between mind and body that is manifested in interest in health food regimes, acupuncture, meditation, and Eastern philosophies. Individuals are inscribing spirituality with, into, and upon the body as part of the gestalt of a healthy life. New Age spirituality is suffused throughout an individual's daily life and identity rather than compartmentalized as a separate set of religious actions or beliefs. The popularity of tattooing and body piercing can be considered a continuation of these trends.

Although those who inflict such alterations upon their bodies often ritualize the process and function within a supportive subcultural group, their actions are not true rituals because they are not part of a fully communally sanctioned and participatory experience, and they do not arise from longstanding cultural traditions. However, although mainstream society may view these actions as transgressing social norms, social norms are changing as bodily self-expression and adornment proliferate and become more accepted. Body alteration is becoming popular as a form of art, communication, and spiritual practice. Self-mutilation, a previously transgressive action, is slowly becoming an accepted, even trendy, method of expressing personal and social messages.

In recent decades, personal style and image cultivation have become more significant as forms of self-expression and indicators of social status. One expresses identity by conforming to the norms of accepted fashion and use of the body, or by rebelling against them. In the early 1960s, body art began as a rebellion in the avant-garde art world. On the streets and in underground clubs in the early 1970s individuals began to mutilate their bodies and flaunt an outrageous subcultural "challenge to hegemony"[8] expressed in a style and music known as punk. Twenty-some years later, this style influences mainstream fashion.

The transgressive uses of the body in both performance art and the youth subculture of the 1970s reveal an intrapsychic dynamic of desire for identity and autonomy similar to the psychological underpinnings of anorexia. Like anorexia these acts are exhibitionist, however they are performed in a social sphere that is deliberately, rather than insidiously, meant to be witnessed. The same is true for tattooing and piercing as expressions of subcultural affiliation. The trajectory of these forms of body alteration from "deviant" to the fashion pages provides insight into the desire for spiritual and social connection, and an American fascination with self-initiation and stigmatization.

Performance Art Breaking the Body Aesthetic

Performance art in which the artist's body is the primary artistic material conveys messages and transforms consciousness by providing alternatives to commonly accepted conventions of time, space, and behavior. Although some critics call performance art a "transgressive ritual,"[9] its marginal position between high culture and low culture and propensity for challenging social norms removes it from the sphere of culturally sanctioned ritual. It is a "liminoid" activity, which Victor Turner defines as a secularized offspring of culturally accepted discourse that grows into a popular or folk culture at the margins of mainstream economic and political practices. It mediates between established and radical discourse. Positioned outside established structures, performance art retains the ability to critique formal social structures, respond to social conflict, and transgress accepted norms. "Liminoid phenomenon are often subversive, representing radical critiques of the central structures and proposing utopian alternative models."[10] One of the factors that contributes to the potential potency of performance art is its accessibility as a form of self-expression for which the artist needs nothing more than his or her body.

As the nineteenth century faded into the twentieth century new attitudes toward the body and its usefulness and beauty as an expressive medium blossomed. The Victorian separation between the body as profane and the spirit as sacred began to change. Isadora Duncan danced in bare feet and bare-legged but was considered chaste as she adamantly explained her dance as a spiritual discourse and her body as territory of the soul. She discarded the corset and confining gowns in favor of a less refined beauty which she associated with the superior harmony of nature and classical Greece. She exemplified an incipient attitude that "the ideal of the expressive body was no longer as a container whose corset-armored skin and neatly circumscribed movements sealed off uncertain and potentially dangerous energies. . . . [The unconstrained body] subverted the dividing line between inner and outer, between the private and public, and in obliterating those boundaries, it held the promise of personal, political, and religious liberation."[11] Tame as Duncan's soulful bare foot seems when placed next to contemporary performance art that aggressively bares and displays not only emotions and the body but the insides of the body as well, at the turn of the century an art that embraced the body and expressed inner desires and emotions was considered revolutionary.

Throughout the twentieth century attitudes toward the body and its representation continued to change. "Primitivism" challenged both previous depictions of the body and the body's kinetic use. Artists and dancers began to reject "civilized" Anglo cultural constriction of the body. The French painter Gauguin went to Tahiti and painted bare-breasted women, Picasso and Derain discovered the magical beauty of African masks, and art movements like Fauvism, Cubism, Expressionism, and Abstract art began to depart from previous methods of representation of the body.[12] Jazz dance in the 1920s manifested a new aesthetic that used the body in ways the demure, symmetrical aesthetics of classical ballet, or even Duncan's flowing aesthetics and pretense of spontaneity, did not. Dances like the Charleston were jerky, sexual, and playful, while dancing to the swing music of the 1930s was energetic, improvised, and syncopated.

Time, events of daily life, and audience participation became significant elements in art of the 1930s, 1940s, and 1950s. Art colonies like Black Mountain cultivated artists such as John Cage and Merce Cunningham who incorporated art into daily life and vice-versa and staged multimedia works as early as 1952.[13] In 1959, Allan Kaprow produced a "Happening," in which randomness and viewer participation were elements of an elastic artistic process, presaging the development of performance art.[13] In the 1960s artists began to place their own bodies in their art and create art that could not be consumed as a commodity. Linda Burnham, who in 1978 founded *High Performance*, a journal of performance art, explains the subversive ideology of the incipient performance art movement.

> Together we created a radical agenda. We made obnoxious art nobody wanted and refused to document it properly. We made performance art nobody could buy or sell. We told gallery owners to fuck off and we refused to hang out with the rich. We lived in the worst neighborhoods and drove the worst cars

and made art out of stuff we found in the street. We even made
art all by ourselves in the middle of nowhere with no audience
. . . for a little while we were free. We thought we were creating
an alternative to elitism, capitalism, materialism, sexism,
racism, jingoism, and most of all careerism.[15]

Rebelling against institutionalization and commercialization,
artists often sensationalized their own bodies. In a 1962 work
entitled "Eye Body," Carolee Schneemann built a loft that contained lights, motorized umbrellas, interlocked panels, and
photos of herself, and placed herself, covered only in ropes, plastic, and chalk, in the space. Schneemann claimed, "Not only am I
image maker, but I explore the value images of flesh as material I
chose to work with. The body may remain erotic, sexual, desired,
desiring, but it is as well votive: marked, written over in text of
stroke and gesture and discovered by my female creative will."[16]
The artistic process, in which unconscious dreams and anxieties
become concrete, is akin to a birthing process that gathers raw
materials and breathes life into them as the artist transforms them
into a work of art. Using her body as one of her materials, the performance artist recreates herself as the new born work of art.

With the act of making oneself a work of art, the artist
reclaims the body, an especially powerful act for women, whose
desires and bodies have often been considered base in the Greco-
Christian tradition. Many performance pieces by women in the
1970s reflected their wish to explore, change, and validate their
daily lives, bodies, and identities. Art as a form of play was also a
form of control. Artists like Eleanor Antin, Lynn Hershmann,
Suzanne Lacy, and Linda Montano created alter egos. Performances by Eleanor Antin and Rachel Rosenthal created personae
and played with assuming and stripping away masks. Continu-
ing to transgress social norms of behavior for women, many
women performers use their bodies to make statements about
socially constructed femininity, gender and sexual roles, and
eroticization of the female body.

Such acts of self-definition and transformation were not performed only by women. Nor were they always benign acts of self-
construction. Vito Acconci burned the hair off his chest and
manipulated his body in an effort to appear more womanly. Ital-
ian artist Gina Pane burned her feet and hands and gashed herself
with a razor during her performances. In one of many works in
which she shed her blood by cutting herself, she outlined her fea-

tures on a mirror into which she was gazing, and then stained the mirror with blood from slits she had made in her eyelids.[17] Mutilating herself and her mirror image visually and metaphorically reproduced and multiplied the artistic product as her bloodshed became both process and product. Her act of self-mutilation and bloodshed was a work of art, which then became a tangible product in which the blood fluid became the ink of the product. Pointing out the extent to which the body and its manipulation is the essence of performance art, Michel Journiac made a pudding with his own blood and offered it for consumption by his audience. He declared, "We may have reached the zero degree of aesthetics and the problem is no longer the beautiful but life itself. In the search for a starting point, the only one for me is my awareness of the body as meat and blood."[18] The sacrifice of human blood for the artistic process echos Christ's sacrifice for the redemption of humankind and exemplifies the artist's willingness to experience pain as a form of self-expression. The artist positions him or herself as the sacrificial scapegoat who will enlighten the audience and save the culture from a fate in which art has become disembodied and insignificant because of its alienation from human life.

Journiac's declaration of the body as a vehicle for expression links these artistic acts with acts of "pathological" self-mutilation. After cutting her arms one self-mutilator said: "These are my arms. I do with them as I please, whenever I please. If I choose to make them ugly, they will be ugly."[19] Comparing her statement with Journiac's underlines the similarity of the two actions as attempts to communicate a plea for control of the body as the most basic material of the art process, communication, and self. An action of self-inflicted pain may be labeled deviant when performed in private, but considered art, albeit perhaps only marginally accepted, when performed for an audience.

As Kathy O'Dell points out in an essay on masochism and performance art, self-injuring acts performed for an audience place the viewer in the uncomfortable position of witnessing and consenting to acts of violence. Gina Pane's performances force the audience to confront "everyday masochisms in which we all engage and upon which we must reflect." Similar to an anorectic who punishes her body to protest her feelings of confinement by family and society, the self-injuring performance artist uses gesture instead of language to convey a message. The message of the performance artist is directed toward society at large. Gina Pane draws her own blood "in the hopes of breaking through the social anesthetization of her audiences, [and] pushing them to think about the violence contained in the everyday imagery that numbed them in the first place."[20] The prison inmate who self-mutilates is attempting to escape the physical and psychological conditions of his imprisonment by inflicting injuries on himself that cannot be denied, just as others who self-harm are attempting to resolve psychological disassociation and alienation and emerge into lucidity. These actions function as attempts to cope with and transcend personal, institutional, and social milieus.

Performance art is a difficult medium to analyze because of the disparities between artist and artwork, authorial intent and received message, but self-mutilatory works often convey messages about spirituality and the gestalt of the flesh fused with the soul. Australian performance artist Stelarc dismisses the idea that his performances create spiritual or social messages, but critics still glean these messages from his work. Stelarc suspends himself in different environments by ropes attached to hooks driven through his flesh, and claims that these works are only "involved with transcending normal human parameters, including pain."[21] Performance artist Rachel Rosenthal offers a more complex interpretation of Stelarc's work as an attempt to "erase the duality of consciousness and physiology in the body through the pain." Basing her analysis on theories of masochism and eradication of the ego, Rosenthal claims Stelarc's actions may be construed as a "metaphysical response to the despair of ever connecting deeply" and an attempt to dissolve the ego or self so thoroughly that a "blissful union with the infinite" is obtained. Rosenthal's interpretation is congruent with both psychological and physiological theories of the effects of self-mutilation as an attempt to achieve both confirmation of a "bounded, masterful self," and a feeling of transcendent connection that obliterates feelings of alienation and fragmentation.

Rosenthal's interpretation moves Stelarc's work to the sphere of public property and cultural drama that does not rely on the artist's statements to construct meaning. Her critical analysis centers on the pain that Stelarc feels rather than the artist as object to be observed. In a public claim for Stelarc's work as "an ordering of violence," Rosenthal expounds upon the virtues of pain and the message that Stelarc's work may convey. "Pain may be a path to orgasm, to the dissolution of the ego, to growth, to understanding, to spiritual enlightenment, moral well-being, and the feeling of being special and superior in culture." Further, according to

Rosenthal, "pain, desired and willed, is metamorphosized into trance, into power, into healing, into apotheosis, into light." Rosenthal's declarations are based on deliberately self-inflicted and consensual pain, and her expansion of Stelarc's view of his work locates his performances in the sphere of cultural drama as social messages that exist independently of authorial intent.[22] These messages rebel against the social taboo against pain and the body as an instrument of ego creation and destruction.

Self-mutilation is a transgressive performance and act of rebellion against modern social norms of body and self because purposefully maiming, defiling, and defacing the human body is a "profanation of humanistic values."[23] Body art and performance liberate both artist and audience because their materials are common to all humans. They are transgressive because they refuse to acknowledge the civilizing norms of a society that has substituted canvas for body, written scripture for body magic, and appropriate appearance as a measure of success. Unconventional use of the body is an attempt to establish independence from socializing restrictions, while the performance of these acts in the public arena is an attempt to engage in social discourse about the transgression of norms. A contemporary example of this is an Austin, Texas, performance group called Flesh Assembly, which stages weekly shows at a local nightclub. Their performances include mock bondage and sadomasochistic rituals, and piercing and force the viewers to confront the eroticism, pain, and modification of the human body presented on stage. In the 1970s, artist Chris Burden performed works in which he locked himself in a locker for several days; punctured, burned, crucified, and chained himself; and had himself run over by a car and shot in the arm. A critic commented, "By operating on his own body, Burden refutes humanism's contract, which assigns to someone else the power to inflict pain, to discipline and examine it, or to place it at risk."[24] The same could be said about performance artist and poet Bob Flanagan whose performances are highly masochistic and incorporate actions from his consensual sadomasochism and autoeroticism. For example, in one of his works he included a video of himself getting his nipples pierced, having his partner cut her initials into his chest, and with his own hands driving a nail through the head of his penis.[25]

Not only do self-mutilators refuse to relinquish the power to self-inflict punishment, they refuse to relinquish the power of self-redemption. To be able to punish, redeem, and transform oneself is to retain one's unique identity and control over it. Acts of self-mutilation implicitly deny the concept of mass salvation through the substitution of Jesus Christ for individual bloodshed. Instead, the individual uses his or her body as a passage to self-transformation. Performance artist Linda Montano confirms the significance of self-transformation as a religious activity when she explains her adolescent eating disorder while living in a convent as an empowering performance emulating holiness. Explaining her inchoate forays into performance art she says, "I appropriated some of Catholicism's mythology—I created my own religion in which I could be what I used to adore; I could start receiving the attention I used to give the saints."[26] Many self-injuring works of performance art parallel the link between suffering and holiness experienced by anorectics that places the performer in the position of being simultaneously the slave under the duress of suffering and discipline and the master inflicting the conditions. The marginal performance artist becomes a self-styled scapegoat who suffers the pangs of social imbalance and communicates them to the audience. The suffering artist becomes both redeemer and redeemed and in the extreme may directly deny the power of an authoritative religious figure to provide redemption. An example from the music arena can be found on Patti Smith's debut album of 1975. Smith, an avant-garde poet, performer, and proto-punk musician, denies that Jesus died for her particular sins in her opening lines of "Gloria,"[27] and casts herself as unredeemed or self-redeemed, and undercuts the idea that Jesus is a savior. Her lyrics repudiating Christian redemption parallel the words of a self-mutilator who carved religious symbols on himself. "I understand that Christ died for everyone but, somehow in my mind, not for me."[28]

Self-mutilation as redemption is the core motivation for performance artist Ron Athey, a gay man who is HIV positive and a former heroin addict. He inserts hypodermic needles into his arm and drives "what looks like a thin knitting needle repeatedly into his forehead, creating an image of a crown of thorns." Although Athey uses Christian references in his performance, he also incorporates African tribal scarring procedures. Athey claims to be exorcising and transcending inner demons with his self-mutilation and inducing an altered consciousness. His performances address involvement in sadomasochistic sex, infection with the HIV virus, "self-loathing, suffering, healing, and redemption." His conflation of self-stigmatization with self-redemption culminates in body art off stage as well via the tribal patterns that tattoo nearly his whole body including his face. Athey asserts he tattooed himself to mark himself as an "outsider."[29] The idea of self-martyrdom will be further explored below.

The action of inflicting pain upon oneself communicates the urgency of the desire for a feeling of spiritual and social connection. By framing an act of self-mutilation as a subversive performance marginally accepted as art, a performance artist can create an identity for him or herself. These artists also communicate a message in the public domain about the spiritual and artistic impoverishment of society and the importance of integrating the body into the discourse in order to combat this impoverishment. As Rudolph Arnheim notes, "Art can present the facts so unmistakably that they often state their demands with more power than they do in daily experience."[30]

Punk Self-Affliction as Social Message

Although they did not call themselves performance artists, punks integrated their self-mutilation and performance of social protest into their daily lives and implicitly declared the street the stage where anyone could display his or her discontent. Their public martyrdom forced a contemplation of the impoverishment of society. As a youth subculture that epitomized hostile rebellion meant to be witnessed, punk can be viewed in several contexts. In part it was a backlash against the groovy-love-peace-hippie idealism of the 1960s.[31] The music was loud and abrasive and the clothes punks wore conjured images of violence and self-mutilation. Although British punks of the late 1970s were members of the working class who were dissatisfied and infuriated with economic stagnation in the United Kingdom, several American musicians foreshadowed the movement in the mid-1960s. The Velvet Underground and Iggy Pop and the Stooges both contributed to the punk sensibility. Patti Smith, the Ramones, the Damned, the New York Dolls, the Buzzcocks, the Clash, and many other groups followed.

The Velvet Underground was one of the first bands to present apocalyptic visions with their aggressive, chaotic music. The performers conveyed an attitude of nihilism and committed stage-presence-suicide by wearing sunglasses and all black clothing, and turning their backs on the audience. Their lyrics were cynical. They experimented with dissonance and semi-predictable electronic feedback in their music. Similar to performance art inclusion of randomness, the Velvets recorded random sounds in their songs, such as a chair being thrown across the room into metal plates.[32] A high performance volume alienated some members of the audience, while thrilling others. While gathering a small group of fans in New York City in the mid-1960s, the Velvet's lack of concern for pleasing the audience and club owners sometimes resulted in losing jobs and getting kicked out of venues. At a 1965 show in Los Angeles the band turned all their amplifiers up after their last song and walked off stage while feedback deafened the audience.[33] In New York City the band sometimes purposefully played songs sure to irritate club owners.[34] Even the band publicity photos made no attempt to be engaging and almost always showed the band staring unsmiling at the camera from behind sunglasses. While pop songs of the time were often celebratory and whimsical in tone, like the Beatles' "Sgt. Pepper" album released in 1967, the Velvet Underground's first album released that same year was cynical and pessimistic in its vision. Rather than contemplating an end to the Vietnam War, an idyllic future, or even the sensual pleasures of romance or recreational drug use, their songs addressed darker social and psychological issues of heroin addiction, domestic violence, cross-dressing, and sado-masochism. One audience member from a 1968 show described the Velvet Underground as creating "an apocalyptic vision of eroticism, sadomasochism, and violence that is at once terrifying and seductive."[35] Instead of pandering to public taste and desire for an optimistic fantasy, the Velvet Underground retreated to an insular world of dark pessimism. By pointing out the sore spots in society, and refusing to polish their music or adhere to standards of performance the Velvets led the way for expression of discontent and the ensuing punk style of that expression.

The Detroit garage band called Iggy Pop and the Stooges also made a "major contribution to the punk aesthetic"[36] with the singer's outrageous stage antics in which he went "beyond performance to the point where it was some kind of psychodrama."[37] Iggy Pop's drama was proto-punk self-mutilation. During a performance on August 29, 1969, Pop cut gashes in his chest with drumsticks, a gesture he repeated with variations thereafter, sometimes using broken bottles, and sometimes rubbing peanut butter in his self-made wounds.[38] These transgressive acts were staged performance art works in which Iggy Pop used his body as his primary material and used self-mutilation to shock the viewer out of complacency by destroying the unity of the human body.

Self-injury as an act of rebellion was later adopted by the Sex Pistols and other punks. Immediately directed toward the audience, but also toward the social arena beyond the performance, self-mutilation expresses nonverbally what the lyrics of many punks songs express bluntly, a crude, in-your-face message of disrespect. Although similar to the Velvet's aloofness and disregard for audience response in its fuck-you message, this attitude confronts the audience head-on. Iggy pop's actions engaged the audience in the punk sensibility by forcing them to participate as witnesses. As punk performance developed it evolved into an even more participatory event.

In ways similar to performance artists, punk rockers manipulated body boundaries and body fluids to communicate messages of chaos and pain. The punk aesthetic of displaying body fluids normally kept inside the body, such as blood, spit and vomit, is an antithesis to the integrity and hygiene of the Western humanist body.[39] By codifying socially unacceptable manners, the punk created a subterranean society and was "determined to cut himself off, to rebuff and drive away normal people, to reserve his allurement for those who override normality, and then add an initiatory ordeal to the labyrinth of allurement."[40]

These punk styles glory in self-stigmatization, and vomit in the face of society while naming that same society as the cause of the nausea. This is exactly what the Sex Pistols did at Heathrow airport on January 4, 1977, when they vomited as one of their many acts of dramatizing the nadir of British society. Engaged in an attempt to achieve disengagement and autonomy, while remaining dependent on social recognition, punks expressed self-abasement as an indirect and subversive method of insulting society. Punk fanzines were replete with self-mockery,[41] and even more potent messages were incarnated in (anti)fashion gestures of tattooing, body piercing, and self-laceration such as carving profane words into one's skin. The goal was to "look as horrifyingly repugnant as possible."[42]

In part, this rebellious stance exhibits a challenge to hegemony via fashion. The most familiar examples of this in America include the tough leather-jacketed youth rebel look of the 1950s, and the scruffy hippie look of the 1960s. However, carving out a unique identity by sporting "indecent" fashions predates even James Dean and Marlon Brando. In *American Beauty*, Lois Banner points out that during the 1850s, middle-class and working-class women began to adopt some of the same styles as prostitutes:

ankle-high skirts and gaudy colors and fabrics. This act was a tacit seizure of fashion power from the upper class which had previously dictated fashionable manners and clothing. In New York City, working-class "Bowery G'Hirls," together with their counterparts the "Bowery B'Hoys," cultivated their own style of dress, speech, and mannerisms and formed what is possibly the first working-class subculture in the United States that was primarily related to economic class and culture rather than to politics or ethnicity.[43] Interestingly, the Bowery B'Hoy seems to foreshadow the British working-class look sometimes associated with a subgroup of punk by adopting suspenders and a black stovepipe hat as distinctive marks of identity. The women challenged Victorian ideals of restrained and quiet femininity by being "loud and hearty." These newly assertive classes rebelled against elite control of fashion,[44] and adopted styles from the underside of society. For instance, the women often wore red boots with their shortened dresses, both of which had previously been considered a sign of prostitution. Their shocking behavior and clothing presaged the punk tactic more than a century later of refusing to conform to fashion dictates from the upper-class, fashion magazines, or even conventional middle-class styles. The Bowery G'Hirl in particular foreshadows the punk girls of later decades as they rebelled against mainstream images of femininity. Punks used their bodies as well as their clothes to usurp fashion power as well as comment on the authority of social codes to dictate their behavior.

As part of a public stance of punk martyrdom, ripped clothes and ripped flesh became symbolic displays of the body as a mutilated product of an impoverished society. The punks' willingness to objectify themselves as repulsive products of their own dissatisfaction and of a sick society, distinguished them from previous performers who expressed bitterness in less dramatic ways. Punks highlighted urban decay by wearing ripped and ragged clothes of soiled cloth, plastic, or other obviously synthetic materials. In opposition to the ideology of cosmetics that are supposed to be unnoticeable except to enhance the beauty of the wearer,[45] and are usually acceptable only for women, both male and female punks self-consciously constructed angry, mocking, and disturbing masks of arched eyebrows, outlined lips, and layer upon layer of face paint. Underneath their outrageous spiked and dyed hair, punks drove safety pins through their ears, lips, and cheeks. As a form of revolt against the greed and affluence of "lard-ass capitalists" the punks cultivated undernourished, emaciated bodies. Punks displayed the paraphernalia of sadomasochism, fetishism, and bondage as a parody and substitute for mainstream ideology of sexuality, consumerism, and fashion. The punks bedecked themselves in "rapist masks and rubber wear, leather bodices and fishnet stockings, implausibly pointed stiletto heeled shoes . . . belts, straps and chains."[46] The subtext of the message was that social rules were akin to a game of dominance and submission, and instead of meekly pretending to be satisfied, punks would display their own revulsion for all to witness. Tricia Henry has linked punk fashion and performance to the mutual audience-performer confrontation and aesthetics of the Russian Futurists, the Dadaists, and the Surrealists. Like these deliberately shocking departures from established art movements, punk rebelled against the status quo. As Daniel Wojcik has cogently described in *Punk and Neo-Tribal Body Art*, a core element of punk was to expose that which society wished to remain hidden, and recontextualize that which society considered polluted or sacred.[47] Punks considered nothing polluted and nothing sacred (Fig. 6).

In his book *Terrorist Chic* Michael Selzer describes punk as a manifestation of social degeneracy. Although he analyzes punk as a manifestation of cultural forces, he insists that it is ultimately meaningless. Selzer depicts contemporary culture as exhibiting a "fascinated approval of violence, brutality, sadomasochism, evil and degeneracy in general; it apotheosizes meaninglessness and indecency." Selzer claims that "degenerate fantasies of sex and violence are not new, [but] making them into a fashionable pose is something of a departure in the history of culture."[48] In his broad critique of the 1970s, Selzer notes the creeping taint of violence and militarism in society, as shown by punks on the street and leather bondage wear and insinuation of violence in fashion spreads. Selzer admits that the brutality that pervades society is meant to be witnessed, but claims it is ultimately an empty spectacle with no motivation or power to make change. According to Selzer, in a culture where there is no "authentic gratification," an audience that gets vicarious pleasure from spectating merely perpetuates the spectacle.

Selzer attributes the reprehensible actions of the real and social "terrorists" he discusses to a deep boredom produced by a society in which everything is "instantly acquirable and instantly disposable." In a society of identity confusion punks are "driven

Fig. 6. Street kids showing punk influence by sporting mohawks and multiple piercings. The woman in the foreground is altering a dress she found in a dumpster. Athough these individuals may not call themselves punks, their survival tactics of using what others have considered trash and their refusal to adhere to standard images of beauty and femininity while adorning their bodies as works of art indicate a marginal stance akin to the one punks assumed in the 1970s. (Photo: John Davis)

to their sensational conduct by their quest for sensation" and aliveness. Selzer uses the metaphor of anorexia to emphasize his point. "The men and women who people the pages of this book are not gluttons but anorectics. The food is there—in fact in abundance unmatched in history—but they cannot get any nourishment from it. Indeed they cannot really eat it."[49]

Although Selzer recognizes the cultural "anorexia of experience" he condemns the punk subculture as perpetuating social degeneracy rather than attempting to display and rectify it. Selzer insists that empty posturing is a core element of punk,[50] and refuses to acknowledge the significance of the masochistic, narcissistic punk stance. Like self-mutilators and anorectics, many punks attempted to establish an identity and awaken their sensations as a response to the environment around them. While Selzer uses an appropriate metaphor of anorectic behavior, he fails to recognize the transcendent potential of the refusal to digest social repast and starve oneself into a state of martyred superiority that horrifies society.

Similar to self-mutilation in other contexts like incarceration or mental distress, punk mutilation is an attempt to express and overcome alienation through subversive attempts to communicate. "Punk wakes people up!" declared *Punk* magazine in 1975. Helen Wheeler, a punk musician, claims punk contributed to her growth and helped her confirm an identity. She says, "No one fucks with me anymore because I've grasped my own integrity and I've taken control and responsibility for myself." Having felt "spiritually dead" in the past, Wheeler claims that during her performances she feels a spiritual awakening. In keeping with both the apocalyptic vision of a numbed and violent society and an effort to transcend that vision and transform herself by self-mutilation, Wheeler cuts herself on stage in a manner she describes as "very ritualistic" and "like a magical pagan act."[51] Performed for her own catharsis, the performance may provide vicarious catharsis for audience members who relate to Wheeler's performance. Her personal ritual becomes a communal ritual as she performs on stage.

Like the masochist who relies on the dominatrix for self-confirmation, or the performance artist who shocks an audience with actions that would be flagrantly unacceptable if performed offstage, the punks wanted a visceral response of repulsion to confirm the effectiveness of their message. Not only did they self-mutilate on stage and in the audience with "broken bottles, fish hooks, and knives," but they vomited, spat, and destroyed the performance area by ripping up seats and throwing items. They reveled in spontaneous self-abuse as the audience and performers exchanged insults. Henry points out that this masochistic activity was a shock tactic used to make a point and gain attention.[52] Like other punk gestures, Iggy Pop's masochistic gesture of rubbing salty peanut butter into his self-inflicted wounds communicates a willingness to go to extremes to feel alive, and rebel against the conventional avenues society presents that are supposed to provide fulfillment. It is a gesture of celebration of the body and its sensations of pain as well as pleasure, and a gesture of anger and self-identification as a victim/Christ-like martyr willing to sacrifice himself to point out the ills of society.

Punks manipulated their appearances as a form of self-creation, social protest, and show of solidarity with victimized and marginalized groups. Punks, who were often white and middle class, strove to marginalize themselves, while ironically declaring themselves victims of a society they claimed classified them as "null." Although the affinity with oppressed groups is overstated, punks claimed it as a motivation for their actions and craved marginal status. Richard Hell, an American proto-punk musician, succinctly claimed "Punks are niggers."[53] Punks expressed their desire for solidarity with stigmatized groups by defacing their appearance and bodies as they recreated themselves as victims who were paradoxically masters of their status and in control of their actions.

By exhibiting their disgust and pain via their clothes, abrasive music, and on their skin the punks commented on "the spiritual paucity of everyday life."[54] By conducting their outrageous acts in public, they engaged in a cathartic social therapy in which they spat, vomited, and bled out the impoverishment and illness of the flawed culture they perceived.

Conclusion

The Cultural Significance of Self-Mutilation

recreate—to give new life or freshness to
recreate—to create again; esp.: to form anew in the imagination
recreation—restoration to health: refreshment of strength and
    spirits after work
                  —*Websters Ninth New Collegiate Dictionary*

In 1969, Edward Podvall noted that "not only does the iconography of self-mutilation appear continually on the landscape of our culture as something seemingly more honest, authentic, pure, or disciplined, but it can be found as an unexpected posture within one particular developmental epoch." He concluded that individual self-mutilation is an attempt to fend off developmental anxiety, and its prevalence may indicate "exoneration and approval by the surrounding culture."[1] As a cultural phenomenon, the iconography of self-mutilation may be interpreted in several ways. Podvall's depiction of self-mutilation as part of a developmental process, like Turner's delineation of body marking as a resolution of an initiation process and like psychoanalytic theory of body narcissism and self-mutilation as attempts to combat fragmentation of the ego, reveals the cultural significance of body modification.

Self-starvation, self-cutting, performance art, and painful, permanent body adornment are potent expressions of rebellion, desire for autonomy, and need to disseminate tension. They are attempts to self-heal, self-initiate, and self-symbolize. Self-mutilation may augment self-awareness, provoke euphoric feelings of spirituality, and resolve a state of liminality by culminating in marks of identity. In the context of culturally sanctioned rituals, these marks incur social inclusion and demarcate social status. In American society, which has considered body alteration practices barbaric and has few formal coming of age rituals that mark the

117

body, the perception of these marks as deviant or perverse has been changing as they have become more common.

Although the extent to which contemporary Western society accepts self-mutilation is debatable, many forms of self-mutilation are becoming increasingly popular as real and symbolic forms of self-creation. The public and private, individual and social spheres in which body alteration is significant are entwined. Self-mutilation cannot be separated from the culture in which it exists. As David Napier points out, American culture is obsessed with "coming of age" as a never-ending process.[2] This struggle to achieve identity is reflected by the implosion of self and identity into the physical symbol, and reality, of the body. The human body is an accessible and viable pathway to holistic integration of self and is a terrain upon which to carve and etch one's deepest desires for identity and meaningful connection to both earthly and spiritual realms. At times altering the body is a form of play and adornment, assuming a mask, playing a role, at other times it is a desperate attempt to feel alive and combat a feeling of alienation and disassociation. Altering the body is an exploration of limits and boundaries of the self, whether in the arena of staged art, subculture, or the local tattoo shop. As individuals test their own limits, they test and change the limits of society.

In a culture that does not order itself with well-defined social and gender roles, religious unity, or coming of age rituals, individuals turn to self-initiation. Self-mutilation becomes a tactic to emerge from psychological fragmentation or disassociation, and integrate one's physical and emotional self. Although individual acts of self-mutilation are problematic because they are not sanctioned by communal rituals or traditions, the physiological effects induced by pain may provoke a feeling of holistic integration. Pain can physiologically alter consciousness by altering brain chemistry and the flow of neuropeptides through the mind/body, while sharpening awareness of body boundaries and self-concept. Pain may induce euphoric feelings of calm well-being, self-mastery, and connection to the surrounding milieu. Anorectics may interpret these feelings as spiritual purity, while self-mutilators may use pain to escape distressing feelings of alienation. Within the institutional setting of prison, self-mutilation and tattooing combat the numbness of the depersonalizing environment and provide a rebellious measure of self-control. As part of this process, pain can provide an avenue of transition from one level of self-awareness to another. Self-mutilators use pain therapeutically to affect a change in consciousness, create a new self, and provide a feeling of self-mastery.

Becoming the Master

In a revealing use of metaphor Bruch explains anorexia as an effort to master the self. She comments that "these girls treat themselves as if they were slave laborers, who are denied all plea-sures and indulgences and are fed a minimum of food and driven to work to the point of physical exhaustion."[3] To cease an eating disorder "the slavelike self-concept must mature."[4] Some anorec-tics use similar imagery to explain their self-imposed starvation. Describing the torment she felt about eating one anorectic com-mented, "I felt as though a slavedriver were whipping me from one activity to the other."[5] The irony in this action is that the suf-ferer enslaves herself. Her skeletal body is expressing a struggle for a psychological and social definition. Anorectic bodies become "living accusations that something [is] painfully wrong."[6] The same is often true for self-mutilators. Even "Bear" Belmares, who has pierced professionally for almost a decade and is well aware of the therapeutic abilities of altering the body, commented about private self-cutting: "there is chaos there."[7] Without a cultural milieu to give these actions meaning, they are private rituals painfully attempting expression to an audience that may or may not listen or understand.

The struggle by the anorectic for recognition and self-mastery functions as a paradigm for other acts of self-mutilation. As Freud points out in *Totem and Taboo*, manipulation of the physical world with special magical procedures to induce psychological effects is an attempt to gain control over internal and the external worlds. Self-mutilation and self-adornment function similarly to these magical procedures. Although imbuing the body with spiritual and magico-religious properties is sometimes considered using the body as a narcissistic self-object, some forms of self-mutilation are less pathologically motivated than others. Some are more commonly called adornment, and incidentally happen to change the body and cause pain. Many people who tattoo and pierce pri-marily enjoy the aesthetic adornment of it. These forms of body modification are often meant to be witnessed as deliberate forms of communication and self-expression. Other body manipulations are meant to convey messages beyond their aesthetic appearance. The blood shed by sufferers of eating disorders, punks, and per-formance artists informs us that something in their environment, whether it be their immediate milieu or the larger social structure, is not satisfying these individuals' human needs. Prisoners tattoo and self-mutilate as an attempt to fulfill needs for identity, stimulus, care, and human connection that are not found in the institutional setting. In reaction to an environment that denies them satisfaction of these needs, they adhere to a subterranean social code, in which they can achieve a kind of substitute social identity and status. Although carving one's flesh is painful, it transforms both self-concept and perception by others. It may transform self-concept by effecting neurochemical changes in the body, as the mystic ascetics discovered. Although most of the body alterations discussed in these pages are not as extreme as some of the tortures self-inflicted by religious martyrs, the instinctive goal of reprogramming the body to effect a change in spirituality is similar. As the individual recreates his or her body, he or she masters consciousness and identity, and perhaps spirituality.

Marginality and Spirituality

Self-inflicted scars, piercings, and tattoos are confessions written on the body as overt or symbolic expressions of self-concept. The marks affiliate the pierced, tattooed, emaciated, or scarred person with a growing segment of the population that rejects cultural norms denying use of the body and self-inflicted pain as vehicles for narcissistic self-confirmation, communication of identity, rebellion, and art. Until the recent mainstream adoption of body modification as fashionable, self-mutilation was an act of self-stigmatization. The appropriation of these behaviors informs us of changing attitudes toward the body, the modern narcissistic need for self-confirmation by others, and the desire to affiliate with marginalized groups.

The spiritual implication of marking the body as a sign of marginality can be metaphorically expressed in the relation between the words *stigma* and *stigmata*. *Stigmata*, meaning the marks resembling the crucifixion wounds of Christ that mysteriously appear upon certain persons,[8] is a derivative of the archaic Greek word for tattoo, which is *stigma*. The Greeks used *stigma* to refer to marks cut or burned upon the body as indicators that the bearer was a criminal, a slave, ritually polluted, or otherwise disgraced or marginal.[9] Stigmata, wounds that appear spontaneously, in replicating the wounds of Christ upon the body are considered marks of Divine recognition. Although marks of deviance inflicted by society marginalize an individual, stigmata that appear by virtue of an individual's grace and holiness elevate as well as marginalize the individual. Stigmata, like other marks upon the body, function as a religious mask that induces a "sacred awe" in both the viewer and the bearer. The body marked with stigmata is considered closer to God and holy grace—the person with stigmata is exposing spirituality via the body and mimicking Christ, whose crucifixion was a supreme act of relinquishing ego while simultaneously differentiating his own spiritual identity. While individuals who modify their own bodies are denying others the right to stigmatize them, they are also refusing to wait for Divine approval to bestow marks of stigmata. A person marked by another is negatively stigmatized, but a person with self-chosen marks of stigmatization transcends social codes of conduct and reifies an intimate connection with the cosmos while communicating a message of individual identity to society. Although contemporary body modifications are not religious stigmata, they have begun to filter into mainstream culture, indicating that American culture has begun to embrace bodily expressions of stigmatized identity (Fig. 7). Although still considered distasteful and nonmainstream by many people, body piercing and tattooing are being adopted by individuals seeking to fulfill spiritual and social identity needs.

In contrast to societies in which body marks are inscribed according to cultural tradition, the self-chosen marks of today's modern cultures are marks of disaffiliation with convention and historical values. Awad Abdelgadir, a native of a small village along the Nile in Sudan, whose facial scars were marked upon him as a child to indicate his tribal identity, explained how his culture's belief in identity is signified by his scars. "I am already made . . . it is scarred into me."[10] He can never forget the traditions of his culture or his identity because a traditional initiation ritual has made them tangible upon his body. In contrast, the tattoos and piercings of the Western world are marks of individuality and serve to create and recreate the individual according to his or her own desires. Each person who chooses to adorn himself or herself with body art chooses a unique mixture of adornments for unique reasons. Although some do eventually consider themselves "finished," others see the process as a lifelong process of "becoming."

Many people with body art mix and match adornments originating in other cultures. They seem to seek a modern "holy grace" of subcultural identity and mind/body holism via painful processes of mutilation and body marking that originate in cultures that have been previously stigmatized. In the eighteenth and nineteenth centuries Native Americans who tattooed and Africans who practiced scarification were considered subhuman. Slaves and prisoners were often physically marked. In the twentieth century tattooing and body piercing have been considered marks of homosexuality and social deviance. All of these connotations of stigma contribute to the iconography of body piercing and tattooing, especially the significance of "neo-tribal" tattoo designs and body modification for women. Nor can we ignore self-mutilation that is considered psychologically aberrant, whether practiced by persons who are formally diagnosed as mentally ill, or by individuals who feel alienated from their surroundings. These individuals instinctively turn to the body as a potent medium of real flesh and blood and as a symbol of the human capacity to interact with his environment. Ornamental body modifications originated in groups considered socially deviant, but has recently become a mark of identity assumed from these marginal groups. The mask of marginalization is the new "sacred awe" that provides the opportunity to rebel, become autonomous from conventional strictures, and create oneself anew within a subcultural milieu. The language of the body cannot be denied. More individuals than ever before want their stories scratched, starved, tattooed, and pierced upon their bodies to be witnessed by society.

The ritualization of self-mutilation contributes to its cultural significance as a form of self-stigmatization. Rene Girard describes rituals, including initiation rituals, as reenactments of previous acts of violence that use a surrogate victim to achieve a communal catharsis.[11] In an effort to order chaos and self-initiate, self-mutilators often ritualize their actions and brand themselves as surrogate victims. The spiritual paucity of modern society is expressed and healed by affiliating with America's wounded subcultures and appropriating rituals and symbols of other cultures. One theorist analyzed Sambian initiation rituals in New Guinea as a lesson in self-stigmatization that strengthens and prepares the initiate for adulthood. "Male initiation, which includes forced nose-bleeding, teaches boys that a master must become like his victim. He must first carry the stigma of what is evil before he obtains the status of a mature person."[12] If we can construct culturally meaningful interpretations of these acts of body adornment, modification, and outright mutilation, instead of commodifying them into empty trends, perhaps we will be on our way to recreating the corpus of society.

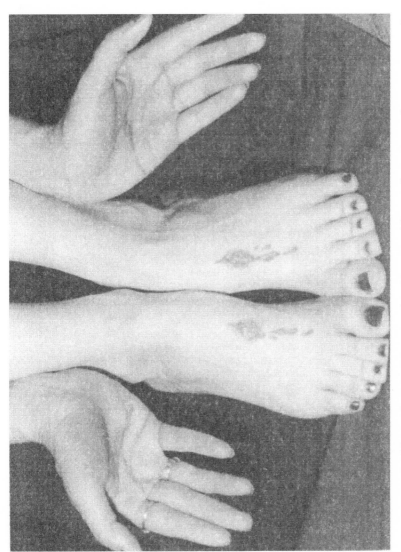

Fig. 7. As part of her religious iconography, Vanessa Alvarez has tattooed stigmata marks upon her hands and feet. (Photo: John Davis)

As David Napier and Mary Douglas have pointed out, the body often symbolizes problems that confront society. Self-mutilating acts are often healing therapies that transform a fragmented self into a whole and mark a passage from an adolescent liminal stage to a fully mature, integrated, and lucid state. In this final stage, the body becomes a revered work of self-determined creativity rather than an object to be destroyed or denied. This reclamation of the body is especially poignant for women. When a woman tattoos or pierces, she is rebelling against gender constrictions, standards of acceptable beauty, and prohibitions on her body. Likewise, punks and artists who self-mutilate are addressing the perceived failures of society. That these actions have become a topic of discussion, common and fashionable, is emblematic of a recognition of the shortcomings of society, and an attempt to transcend them. The popularity of self-mutilatory acts expresses the American struggle to achieve spirituality and social identity, establish individuality and autonomy, and reify a culture in which coming of age is marked by becoming like the victim.

Finally, as individuals modify their bodies as exploration of their individual identities, the culture composed of these individuals begins to explore what it means to be human and what role the body plays in civilization. The realization that manipulation of the body is part of a process that allows individuals to emerge into chosen identities and transcend past events, social standards and everyday consciousness prompts the question "what are the limits of human self-creation?" As technology advances to the point where one can consider genetic recreation of the body, new dilemmas for recreating the self and society through artificial—and artistic—means will appear. The urge to expand human power to create and re-create will find new avenues that will challenge social definitions of marginality.

Notes

Introduction

1. Louise J. Kaplan, *Female Perversions: The Temptations of Emma Bovary* (New York: Doubleday, 1991). As Kaplan lists them, these include "tweezings, depilations, starvation diets, hair cuttings, hair permings, hair straightenings, facial scrubs and acid abrasions, nail whittlings and cuticle trimmings, liposuctions, excisions of bony tissue, breast jobs and hip jobs and nose jobs" (366). A look at the history of women's fashions illuminates even more examples of women altering their physical being in response to the fetishizing of their bodies. These actions may also be interpreted as an individual's initiating herself into the socially acceptable being that is construed as a sexually mature adult.

2. Kaplan, 9-15.

Chapter 1

1. Maurice Merleau-Ponty, *Phenomenology of Perception*, trans. Colin Smith (New York: Humanities Press, 1962), 150-51.

2. Holger Kalweit considers the essential field of study the study of consciousness and its variations, especially "states of consciousness that for us smack of irrationality, hysteria, pathology, and myth but that other cultures regard as vivifying and existentially important." *Shamans, Healers, and Medicine Men* (Boston: Shambhala, 1992), 260.

3. Sigmund Freud, "Animism, Magic and the Omnipotence of Thoughts," *Totem and Taboo* (New York: W.W. Norton, 1931), 97.

4. Freud, 98.

5. Freud, 112.

6. Albert J. Raboteau, *Slave Religion: The "Invisible" Institution in the Antebellum South* (New York: Oxford University Press, 1978), 269, 286-87.

7. Freud, 105.

8. Freud, 113.

9. Susan Vogel, "Baule Scarification: The Mark of Civilization," *Marks of Civilization: Artistic Transformations of the Human Body*, ed. Arnold Rubin (Los Angeles: Museum of Cultural History, University of California, 1988), 97-105.

10. Two articles were very helpful in helping me understand how masks function as a bridge between the spiritual and physical worlds, particularly in Yoruba *Egungun* ceremonies: Margaret Thompson

Drewal, "Portraiture and Construction of Reality in Yorubaland and Beyond," *African Arts* 23.3 (1990): 40-49; and Allen F. Roberts, "Tabwa Masks: An Old Trick of the Human Race," *African Arts* 23.2 (1990): 36-47.

11. Michel Thevoz, *The Painted Body: Illusions of Reality* (New York: Rizzoli, 1984), 34.

12. See figures page 189, in Joy Gritton, "Labrets and Tattooing in Native Alaska," *Marks of Civilization*, ed. Arnold Rubin (Los Angeles: Museum of Cultural History, University of California, 1988), 181-90.

13. Desmond Morris, "Body Adornment: Social Mutilations and Cosmetic Decorations," *Dimensions of Dress and Adornment: A Book of Readings*, ed. Lois M. Gurel and Marianne S. Beeson, 3rd ed. (Dubuque, Iowa: Kendall/Hunt, 1975), 18.

14. Thevoz, 119.

15. Mikhail Bakhtin, *Rabelais and His World*, trans. Helene Iswolsky (Bloomington: Indiana University Press, 1984), 24-30.

16. Mary Douglas, *Purity and Danger: An Analysis of the Concepts of Pollution and Taboo* (London: Ark Paperbacks, 1966), 138.

17. Thevoz, 25.

18. Mary Douglas, *Natural Symbols: Explorations in Cosmology* (New York: Random Books, 1970), 93-112.

19. Douglas, *Natural Symbols*, 104.

20. Maya Deren quoted in Holger Kalweit, *Shamans, Healers, and Medicine Men*, trans. Michael H. Kohn (Boston: Shambhala, 1992), 69, 134.

21. Timothy Leary, Ralph Metzner, and Richard Alpert, *The Psychedelic Experience: A Manual Based on the Tibetan Book of the Dead* (New York: Carol Publishing Group, 1962). Although too lengthy to expound upon here, the comparison between the neurochemistry of chemically induced altered states and altered states induced by fasting, chanting, meditation, or dancing would make a fascinating study.

22. Alfred C. Haddon, *Magic and Fetishism* (London: Archibald Constable, Ltd., 1906), 2-3.

23. James Frazer, *The New Golden Bough* (New York: New American Library, 1964), 62-70.

24. Eli Sagan, *Cannibalism: Human Aggression and Cultural Form* (New York: Harper, 1974), 9, 33.

25. Holger Kalweit, *Shamans*, 75-78.

26. Douglas, *Purity and Danger*, 114-28.

27. Tomas Agosin, "Psychosis, Dreams and Mysticism in the Clinical Domain," *The Fires of Desire: Erotic Energies and the Spiritual Quest*, ed. Frederica Halligan and John J. Shea (New York: Crossroad Publishing, 1992), 61.

28. Henry John Drewal and Margaret Thompson Drewal, *Gelede: Art and Female Power among the Yoruba* (Bloomington: Indiana University Press, 1990), 5-6.

29. Agosin, 61.

30. Thevoz, 19.

31. W.D. Hambly, *The History of Tattooing and Its Significance* (London: H.F. & G. Witherby, 1925), 240.

32. Thevoz, 12.

33. Konrad Spindler, *The Man in the Ice: The Discovery of a 5,000-Year-Old Body Reveals the Secrets of the Stone Age* (New York: Harmony Books, 1994), 167-72.

34. Thevoz, 34.

35. Sterling Eisminger, "The Curious Disposition of Body Parts, 1800-1850: Coincidence of Romantic Impulse?" *The Stiffest Corpse*, ed. Andrei Codescu (San Francisco: City Lights Books, 1989), 222-24.

36. M.P. Pandit, *Gems from the Tantras: Kularnava* (India: Ganesh, 1975), 3.

37. Georg Feuerstein, *Yoga: The Technology of Ecstasy* (Los Angeles: Jeremy P. Tarcher, 1989), 250-54. Miranda Shaw, *Passionate Enlightenment: Women in Tantric Buddhism* (Princeton: Princeton University Press, 1994), 20-27.

38. Rudolph M. Bell, *Holy Anorexia* (Chicago: University of Chicago Press, 1985), 22-53.

39. Amanda Porterfield, *Female Piety in Puritan New England: The Emergence of Religious Humanism* (New York: Oxford University Press, 1992), 143-53.

40. Bordo quoted in Scott Heller, "Philosopher Links Classical Texts and 'Vogue' Models in a Study of Cultural Pressures on Women and Their Bodies," *Chronicle of Higher Education*, 8 September 1993: A10, A16. See also Susan Bordo, "Anorexia Nervosa: Psychopathology as the Crystallization of Culture," *Feminism and Foucault: Reflections on Resistance*, ed. Irene Diamand and Lee Quimby (Boston: Northeastern University Press, 1988), 92. Bordo's most recent book, an extensive cultural analysis of eating disorders, is titled *Unbearable Weight: Feminizing Western Culture and the Body* (Berkeley: University of California Press, 1992).

41. John A. Sours, *Starving to Death in a Sea of Objects: The Anorexia Syndrome* (New York: Jason Aronson, 1980), 226.

42. Frances E. Mascia-Lees and Patricia Sharpe, eds., *Tattoo, Torture, Mutilation, and Adornment: The Denaturalization of the Body in Culture and Text* (Albany: State University of New York Press, 1992), 3.

43. Philip Rieff, *The Triumph of the Therapeutic: Uses of Faith after Freud* (Chicago: University of Chicago Press, 1987), 11.

44. Norbert Elias, *The Civilizing Process: The History of Manners,* trans. Edmund Jephcott (New York: Urizen Books, 1978), 78-79.

45. Elias, 200-03.

46. Elias, 138-39.

47. I would argue, however, that by taking a right-wing, hard-core stance against pornography, some contemporary feminists are depriving both men and women of their right to control and enjoy their bodies.

48. Christopher Lasch, *The Culture of Narcissism* (New York: W.W. Norton, 1979), 91.

49. Bernard Rudofsky, *The Unfashionable Human Body* (Garden City: Anchor Press, 1974), 35.

50. Rudofsky, 212.

51. Heinz Kohut, *The Restoration of the Self* (New York: International Universities Press, 1977), 63-93.

52. Kohut, 117-38.

53. A. Sugarman and C. Karash, "The Body as Transitional Object in Bulimia," *International Journal of Eating Disorders* 1 (1982): 57-67.

54. Karl M. Abenheimer, "On Narcissism," *Narcissism, Nihilism, Simplicity and Self* (Edinburgh: Aberdeen University Press, 1991), 53-58.

55. Abenheimer, 57.

56. David W. Krueger, *Body Self and Psychological Self: A Developmental and Clinical Integration of Disorders of the Self* (New York: Brunner/Mazel, 1989), 58.

57. Krueger, 102.

58. Krueger, 79.

59. Philip Cushman, "Why the Self Is Empty: Toward a Historically Situated Psychology," *American Psychologist* 45.5 (1990): 599-611.

Chapter 2

1. Steven F. Brena, *Pain and Religion: A Psychophysiological Study* (Springfield: Charles C. Thomas, 1972), 5.

2. Brena, 132.

3. Aldous Huxley, *The Doors of Perception and Heaven and Hell* (1955; New York: Harper, 1963), 67, 88. Discussion of biological causes of visionary experience, 133.

4. David Bodanis, *The Body Book: A Fantastic Voyage to the World Within* (Boston: Little, Brown, 1984), 44-63, 203.

5. Bodanis, 166.

6. Joseph Previte, *Human Physiology* (New York: McGraw Hill, 1983), 251.

7. Harris Dienstfrey, *Where the Mind Meets the Body* (New York: HarperCollins, 1991), 91-108.

8. Previte, 251.

9. Janice M. Cauwels, *Bulimia: The Binge-Purge Compulsion* (Garden City: Doubleday, 1983), 167-74.

10. Andrew Weil, *The Marriage of the Sun and the Moon: A Quest for Unity in Consciousness* (Boston: Houghton Mifflin, 1980), 8-14. Weil discusses many different foods and rituals that he claims promote physical euphoria and are sometimes used as steppingstones to elevated awareness and spiritual experience.

11. Kaplan, 466.

12. Hilde Bruch, *The Golden Cage: The Enigma of Anorexia Nervosa* (Cambridge: Harvard University Press, 1978). Bruch discusses the psychological and physiological effects of prolonged fasting, 1-21. She posits that medieval religious visions may have been caused by the physical effects of fasting, 18.

13. Kalweit, 102.

14. Armando R. Favazza and Barbara Favazza briefly overview myths and practices of self-mutilation in religions around the world in "Self-Mutilation in Myths of Creation, Shamanism, and Religion" in *Bodies Under Siege: Self-Mutilation in Culture and Psychiatry* (Baltimore: Johns Hopkins University Press, 1987), 23-44. Another very informative, succinct overview is provided by Karl Menninger, "A Psychoanalytic Study of the Significance of Self-Mutilation," *Psychoanalytic Quarterly* 4.3 (1935): 408-66.

15. William James, *The Varieties of Religious Experience* (1902; New York: New American Library, 1958), 238.

16. James, 241.

17. Kalweit, 108.

18. Elaine Scarry, *The Body in Pain: The Making and Unmaking of the World* (New York: Oxford University Press, 1985), 27-38. Scarry discusses the use of torture to strip away dignity and self-expression.

19. Roy F. Baumeister, *Masochism and the Self* (Hillsdale: Lawrence Erlbaum Associates, 1989), 31.

20. Baumeister, 85.

21. Quoted in Sono Motoyama, "Hurts So Good: Whips, Chains, and Nipple Clamps—and the Nice Folks Next Door Who Use Them," *Baltimore City Paper* 17.3 (15 January 1992): 10.

22. Sheila S. Walker, *Ceremonial Spirit Possession in Africa and Afro-America: Forms, Meanings and Functional Significance for Individuals and Social Groups* (Leiden, Netherlands: E.T. Brill, 1972), 18.

23. See pages 290-91 in Jessica Benjamin, "Master and Slave: The Fantasy of Erotic Domination," *Powers of Desire: The Politics of Sexuality*, ed. Ann Snitow and Christine Stansell (New York: Monthly Review Press, 1983), 280-99.

24. Edward M. Podvall, "Self-Mutilation Within a Hospital Setting: A Study of Identity and Social Compliance," *British Journal of Medical Psychology* 42.3 (1969): 213.

25. Valerie Steele, *Fetish: Fashion, Sex, and Power* (New York: Oxford University Press, 1996), 193.

26. Steele, 169-72. Steele explores the subtleties of power shown by fetish fashions in sadomasochistic interactions. The slave may remain naked or near naked as a sign of inferiority, vulnerability, or access to the dominator's desires, while the dominator is often "heavily-armored."

27. Jacob Bilmes and Alan Howard, "Pain as Cultural Drama," *Anthropology and Humanism Quarterly* 5 (1980): 10.

28. Robert N. Bellah et al. *Habits of the Heart: Individualism and Commitment in American Life* (Berkeley: University of California Press, 1985), 130.

29. Joseph L. Henderson, *Thresholds of Initiation* (Middletown: Wesleyan University Press, 1967), 14.

30. Francis Amery, "Self-Sacrifice," *The Dedalus Book of Femme Fatales*, ed. Bruce Stableford (Cambs, U.K.: Dedalus, 1992), 244.

31. David A. Napier, *Foreign Bodies: Performance, Art, and Symbolic Anthropology* (Los Angeles: University of California Press, 1992), 32.

32. Arnold Van Gennep, *The Rites of Passage*, trans. Monika B. Vizedon and Gabrielle L. Caffee (Chicago: University of Chicago Press, 1960), 68-71.

33. Victor Turner, *The Ritual Process: Structure and Anti-Structure* (Chicago: Aldine, 1969), 103-12. Rene Girard, *Violence and the Sacred*, trans. Patrick Gregory (Baltimore: Johns Hopkins University Press, 1977), 280-84. Comparing the silence, humility, and obedience of the liminal entity to the role of the submissive person in a sadomasochistic interaction would be a fascinating study that might illuminate the ways in which sadomasochistic interactions provide identity.

34. Walker, 29.

35. Victoria Ebin, *The Body Decorated* (London: Blacker, Calmann Cooper, 1979), 27. See also Mircea Eliade, *Rites and Symbols of Initiation: The Mysteries of Birth and Rebirth*, trans. Willard R. Trask (New York: Harper, 1958).

36. Douglas, 174.

37. Van Gennep, 71-72.

38. Henderson, 232.

Chapter 3

1. Favazza and Favazza, 233-34.

2. Because eating disorders most frequently affect women, and for the sake of simplicity, I use the feminine pronoun in this chapter. American research shows the prevalence of anorexia to be about 1 case per 100 adolescent girls. Bulimia seems to occur more frequently and in 1989 was reported to affect from 1.9 to 4 percent of all women. The female college population is most at risk for partaking in bulimic behavior. Alayne Yates, "Current Perspectives on the Eating Disorders: I. History, Psychological and Biological Aspects," *Journal of the American Academy of Child and Adolescent Psychology* 28.6 (1989): 815. More recently, Dr. Darlene Atkins, director at the eating disorders clinic at the Children's National Medical Center in Washington estimated that while 1 percent of American girls and women suffer from anorexia, 19 percent have bulimia, and a much higher percentage suffer subclinical eating disorders in which they experience disruption in their lives from eating problems even though the symptoms may not be diagnosed as a full-fledged disorder. Dawn Margolis, "By Food Obsessed," *American Health* 15.3 (1996): 47.

3. Stephen Mennell, *All Manners of Food: Eating and Taste in England and France from the Middle Ages to the Present* (Oxford: Basil Blackwell, 1985), 38. Mennell presents a sociocultural history of cookery and diet.

4. John Money, "The Diet That Cured Sex," *The Destroying Angel: Sex, Fitness and Food in the Legacy of Degeneracy Theory, Graham Crackers, Kellogg's Corn Flakes and American Health History* (Buffalo: Prometheus Books, 1985), 17-26.

5. Joan Jacob Brumberg, *Fasting Girls: The Emergence of Anorexia Nervosa as a Modern Disease* (Cambridge: Harvard University Press, 1988), 175-82.

6. Abba Goold Woolson, *Woman in American Society* (Boston: Roberts Brothers, 1873).

7. T.J. Jackson Lears, *No Place of Grace: Antimodernism and the Transformation American Culture, 1880-1920* (New York: Pantheon, 1981), 32.

8. Brumberg discusses the details of the cases of Sarah Jacobs, Molly Fancher, and other cases of fasting girls and the attempts by the medical community to verify prolonged fasts as fraudulent, while proponents of the popular urban Spiritualist movement interpreted fasting as a quest for transcendence of the material body, 62-91.

9. Brumberg, 118-29.

10. Yates, 816. Yates notes that minority women are more likely to develop eating disorders as they depart from traditional values that may include different aesthetics for the female form. This may also be related to a desire for independence and autonomy.

11. See Brumberg, 3, 12-13. Brumberg cites an incidence of 1.6 cases of eating disorders per 100,000 members of the general population, 12. The book is an extensive history of eating disorders as a product of modern medicalization and secularization. Brumberg concludes in part that anorexia is a manifestation of perfectionism and an effort at personal salvation via control over one's body.

12. Brumberg, 14.

13. Yates notes that "throughout history, anoretic behaviors have been closely linked to religious exercises designed to enable the conquest of the body or the spirit. Through mortification of the flesh, an individual gains spiritual liberation, [and] a merger of the self with God" (813-14). There is a strong connection between anorectic and bulimic behaviors, with almost half of the individuals diagnosed with anorexia exhibiting bulimic behavior. Between 30 and 80 percent of bulimic individuals have a history of anorectic behavior.

14. Guido Majno, *The Healing Hand: Man and the Wound in the Ancient World* (Cambridge: Harvard University Press, 1975), 129.

15. Majno, 179.

16. Bell, 43.

17. Bell, 22-53.

18. See Robert L. Moore, "Decoding the Diamond Body: The Structure of the Deep Masculine and the Forms of the Libido," *The Fires of Desire: Erotic Energies and the Spiritual Quest,* ed. Frederica R. Halligan and John J. Shea (New York: Crossroad Publishing), 112.

19. Yates, 816. Yates cites a 1970 study by C. Rowland as the source of this information.

20. A. Goodsitt, "Self-Regulatory Disturbances in Eating Disorders," *International Journal of Eating Disorders* 2 (1983): 51-60.

21. Sours, 226.

22. Bruch, 9-10, 84-85.

23. Bruch, 1-21; Sours, 226.

24. Sours, 226.

25. Sheila MacLeod, *The Art of Starvation: A Story of Anorexia and Survival* (New York: Schocken, 1982). Macleod claims that her stringent eating habits were an attempt to prove her superiority, pureness, and control over her body. "The apparent text of my behavior, openly declared, read 'I am superhuman. I don't need food'" (71). See also Bruch, 16.

26. Judith Rodin, *Body Traps: Breaking the Binds That Keep You from Feeling Good About Your Body* (New York: William Morrow, 1992), 172.

27. Quoted in Madeleine Pelner Cosman, *Fabulous Feasts: Medieval Cookery and Ceremony* (New York: George Braziller, 1976), 109. Years later,

the Marquis de Sade echoed Aquinas: "There is no passion more closely involved with lechery than drunkenness and gluttony" (quoted in Kaplan, 355).

28. Fasting was acceptable if it was deemed to exemplify the power of the church to govern behavior. Church authorities did not necessarily approve of obviously self-willed acts of denial. If the fast became prolonged or was accompanied by extreme behavior or claims to holiness, Church officials often interpreted it as a threat to church authority and commanded that it cease. In *Holy Anorexia* Bell points out several examples of this power struggle in his discussion of female saints.

29. Hillel Schwartz, *Never Satisfied: A Cultural History of Diets, Fantasies, and Fat* (New York: Free Press, 1986), 9-11.

30. Cosman, 103-23.

31. R.F. Kandel and G.H. Pelto, "The Health Food Movement: Social Revitalization or Alternative Health Maintenance System?" *Nutritional Anthropology: Contemporary Approaches to Diet and Culture*, ed. N.W. Jerome et al. (Pleasantville: Redgrave, 1980), 328-63.

32. Bruch, 4, 42-43.

33. Because the anorectic is "poorly equipped to meet the challenge of establishing autonomy and an independent identity . . . she establishes a sense of mastery by controlling her body through diet" (Yates 819). The body may be both the battlefield for conflict and one of the sources of the conflict. "Body image is so crucial to a person's core of identity, psychologists believe, that distortions in it can have significant effects that we should all watch out for. They can be as benign as just affecting our mood or as serious as creating a susceptibility to a range of psychological problems, particularly depression" (Rodin 57).

34. Maud Ellmann, *The Hunger Artists: Starving, Writing, and Imprisonment* (Cambridge: Harvard University Press, 1993), 2.

35. Kim Chernin, *The Hungry Self: Women, Eating, and Identity* (New York: Times Books, 1985), 17.

36. MacLeod, 56.

37. Yates, 814.

38. Weil, 14-18.

39. Susie Orbach, *Hunger Strike: The Anorectic's Struggle As a Metaphor for Our Age* (New York: W.W. Norton, 1986), 16.

40. Weil, 14-18.

41. "[H]eightened awareness of the body can serve as a means to more integrated body experience and self-knowledge, and as an anchorage point to reality." Douwe Tiemersma, *Body Schema and Body Image: An Interdisciplinary and Philosophical Study* (Amsterdam: Swets & Zeitlinger, 1989), 100.

42. Kalweit, 30-34.

43. Yates, 819. Yates references this idea to a study by W. Swift and R. Letven in 1984.

44. Yates, 821. Yates references this to a 1988 study by Fullerton et al.

45. Rodin, 86.

46. Yates, 819.

47. MacLeod, 67.

48. Kaplan, 461.

49. MacLeod, 70.

50. Chernin, 93. Chernin discusses individual epidemiology and the bond between mother and daughter as important to acceptance of a mature female body, and discusses the anorectic's desire for androgyny as a cultural product, 189-94.

51. Chernin, 168.

52. Chernin, 167.

53. Marion Woodman, *Addiction to Perfection: The Still Unravished Bride* (Toronto: Inner City Books, 1982), 82.

54. Morag MaSween, *Anorexic Bodies: A Feminist and Sociological Perspective in Anorexia Nervosa* (New York: Routledge, 1993), 243.

55. Kohut, 128.

56. John S. Kafka, "The Body as a Transitional Object: A Psychoanalytic Study of a Self-Mutilating Patient," *British Journal of Medical Psychology* 42 (1969): 207.

57. E. Sue Blume, "The Walking Wounded: Post-Incest Syndrome," *Siecus Report* 15.1 (1986): 6.

58. Within the general population women self-mutilate more frequently than men in a ratio of 1.5: 1. For this reason and for the sake of simplicity, I will use the feminine pronoun when discussing self-mutilation in the general population. See Steven J. Shea and Mary Craig Shea, "Self-Mutilatory Behavior in a Correctional Setting," *Corrective and Social Psychiatry and Journal of Behavior Technology Methods and Therapy* 37.4 (1991): 65.

59. A.T., Personal communication April 13, 1994.

60. Takao Mukai, "A Call for Our Language: Anorexia from Within," *Women's Studies International Forum* 12.6 (1989): 613-38. Mukai's autobiographical essay provides insight to many of the issues discussed here, ranging from ritualization of eating disorders to skin eroticism to differentiating body boundaries and sense of self.

61. Orbach, 16-17.

62. Favazza and Favazza, 198-99; Kaplan, 383.

63. Of course not all acts of ritualized self-abuse are cut off from culturally sanctioned meanings, for example religious penitents in the

Southwest still practice ritual self-flagellation. See Marta Weigle, *Brothers of Light: Brothers of Blood: The Penitents of the Southwest* (Albuquerque: University of New Mexico Press, 1976), 188, 285.

64. Favazza and Favazza, 44.

65. Kaplan, 383.

66. Napier, 173.

67. Orbach, 102.

68. Orbach, 157.

69. Kaplan, 367-68.

70. Bakhtin, 24-30.

71. Napier, 173.

72. Favazza and Favazza, 205.

73. Armando R. Favazza and Karen Conterio, "The Plight of Chronic Self-Mutilators," *Community Mental Health Journal* 24.1 (1988): 29.

74. Favazza and Conterio, "Plight," 78.

75. Favazza and Conterio, "Plight," 78.

76. Kaplan, 367.

77. Menninger, "Psychoanalytic Study," 408-66. See also Menninger's *Man Against Himself* (New York: Harcourt Brace, 1938).

78. Tepilit Ole Saitoti, *The Worlds of a Maasai Warrior: An Autobiography* (New York: Random House, 1986), 67. See also Cheryl Bentsen, *Maasai Days* (New York: Summit Books, 1989), 204-17.

79. Many of the mutilatory practices of non-Western cultures are controversial because of their motivation and method of enforcement, as discussed by Alice Walker and Prathiba Parmar in their book *Warrior Marks: Female Genital Mutilation and the Sexual Blinding of Women* (New York: Harcourt Brace, 1993).

80. Favazza and Conterio, "Plight," 22-23.

81. Shea and Shea, 64-67.

82. Stanley Cohen and Laurie Taylor, *Psychological Survival: The Experience in Long-Term Imprisonment* (New York: Pantheon, 1972), 41-59.

83. See Ann Cordilia, *The Making of an Inmate: Prison as a Way of Life* (Cambridge: Schenkman, 1983).

84. Hans Toch, *Living in Prison: The Ecology of Survival* (New York: Free Press, 1977), 21-37.

85. Cohen and Taylor, 57.

86. Toch, *Living in Prison*, 48.

87. Elmer H. Johnson and Benjamin Britt, *Felon Self-Mutilation: Correlate of Stress in Prison* (Carbondale: Center for the Study of Crime, Delinquency and Corrections, Southern Illinois University, 1969), 22-63.

88. Hans Toch, *Men in Crisis: Human Breakdowns in Prison* (Chicago: Aldine, 1975), 6.

89. "Correctional Architecture: The Symptoms of Neglect, The Signs of Hope," *Architectural Record* 150 (August 1971): 111.

90. U.S. Bureau of Prisons, *Recent Prison Construction 1950-1960* (U.S. Bureau of Prisons, 1960), 28.

91. Shea and Shea, 66.

92. Shea and Shea, 66.

93. Toch, *Men in Crisis*, 46.

94. Robert Robertson Ross and Hugh Bryan McKay, *Self-Mutilation* (Lexington: Lexington Books, 1979), 107.

95. Shea and Shea, 65.

Chapter 4

1. Herman Melville, *Moby Dick; or the Whale* (Berkeley: University of California Press, 1979), 490.

2. Henry David Thoreau, *Walden and Civil Disobedience* (1854; New York: Penguin Books, 1983), 69.

3. Menninger, "Psychoanalytic Study," 408-66.

4. A.T. Sinclair, "Tattooing—Oriental and Gypsy," *American Anthropologist* 10.3 (1908): 361-86.

5. John Carswell, *Coptic Tattoo Designs* (Beirut: American University of Beirut, 1958), xv-xxii.

6. Samuel M. Steward, *Bad Boys and Tough Tattoos: A Social History of the Tattoo with Gangs, Sailors, and Street-Corner Punks, 1950-1965* (New York: Harrington Park Press, 1990), 79.

7. Thevoz, 7.

8. Thevoz, 8.

9. Albert Parry, *Tattoo: Secrets of a Strange Act as Practised among the Natives of the United States.* (New York: Simon & Schuster, 1933), 1-2.

10. Robert S. Bianchi. "Tattoo in Ancient Egypt," *Marks of Civilization* (Los Angeles: Museum of Cultural History, University of California, 1988), 21-28. Bianchi discusses the origins and significance of tattooing in Egypt.

11. Hambly, 315.

12. Arnold Rubin, "Introduction: Asia," *Marks of Civilization* (Los Angeles: Museum of Cultural History, University of California, 1988), 107.

13. Steward, 187-88.

14. Sinclair, 374.

15. Hambly, 236-37.

16. Irving Goldman, *Ancient Polynesian Society* (Chicago: University of Chicago Press, 1970), 256. See also E.S. Craighill Handy and Wil-

lowdean Chatterson Handy, *Samoan House Building, Cooking, and Tattooing*, Bulletin 15 (Honolulu: Bernice P. Bishop Museum, 1924).

17. Hambly, 55-56.

18. Awad Abdelgadir, interview by author, 19 March 1996, Austin, Texas. Awad Abdelgadir was born in a village of 200 inhabitants along the Nile in Northern Sudan. Although he received facial scarring during his initiation into manhood about thirty years ago, he claims his village no longer practices scarification.

19. Douglas W. Light, *Tattooing Practices of the Cree Indians* Occasional Paper No. 6 (Calgary: Glenbow Alberta Institute), 11-13.

20. Mircea Eliade, *Birth and Rebirth: The Religious Meanings of Initiation in Human Culture*, trans. Williard Trask (New York: Harper, 1958), 18, 31, 43.

21. Steward, 186.

22. Thevoz, 67.

23. Nancy A. Gutierrez, "Philomela Strikes Back: Adultery and Mutilation as Female Self-Assertion," *Women's Studies* 16 (1989): 429-43.

24. Parry, *Tattoo: Secrets of a Strange Act*, 123.

25. Light, 19.

26. William D. Piersen, *Black Legacy: America's Hidden Heritage* (Amherst: University of Massachusetts Press, 1993), 83.

27. Henry John Drewal, "Beauty and Being: Aesthetics and Ontology in Yoruba Body Art," *Marks of Civilization* (Los Angeles: Museum of Cultural History, University of California, 1988), 83-96.

28. Orlando Patterson, *Slavery and Social Death: A Comparative Study* (Cambridge: Harvard University Press, 1982), 58-59.

29. Thevoz, 64-65.

30. Parry, *Tattoo: Secrets of a Strange Art*, 59.

31. See Eric Lott, *Love and Theft: Blackface Minstrelsy and the American Working Class* (New York: Oxford University Press, 1993).

32. Clinton Sanders, *Customizing the Body: The Art and Culture of Tattooing* (Philadelphia: Temple University Press, 1989), 16.

33. Sanders, *Customizing the Body*, 18-19.

34. Albert Parry, "Tattoo Crisis," *Stories of Tramp Life*, ed. E. Haldeman-Julius, Little Blue Book No. 1412. (Girard: Haldeman-Julius Publications, 1929), 50-57.

35. Parry, *Tattoo: Secrets of a Strange Art*, 112.

36. Parry, *Tattoo: Secrets of a Strange Art*, 22-27.

37. Parry, "Tattoo Crisis," 52. *Tattoo: Secrets of a Strange Art*, 27.

38. Albert Parry, "Tattooing among Prostitutes and Perverts," *Psychoanalytic Quarterly* 3 (1934): 476-82.

39. J. Lander and H.M. Kohn, "A Note on Tattooing Among Selectees," *American Journal of Psychiatry* 100 (1943): 326-27.

40. R.S. Post, "The Relation of Tattoos to Personality Disorder," *Journal of Criminal Law, Criminology, & Police Science* 59.4 (1968): 516-24.

41. A.J.W. Taylor, "Tattooing among Male and Female Offenders of Different Ages in Different Types of Institutions," *Genetic Psychological Monographs* 81.1 (1970): 81-119.

42. Taylor, 112-14.

43. R.E. Hawkins and J.A. Popplestone, "The Tattoo as Exoskeletal Defense," *Perceptual and Motor Skills* 19.2 (1964): 500. This study surveyed 556 subjects.

44. Robert J. Stoller, *Pain and Passion: A Psychoanalyst Explores the World of S&M* (New York: Plenum Press, 1991), 24.

45. Richard Pierce, "Tattooed Doll," *New York Times Magazine* 25 June 1995, 18.

46. One such exhibit, titled "Skin as Landscape," was shown at St. Lawrence University in Canton, New York, in February 1995. Another exhibit, titled "Pierced Hearts and True Love: A Century of Drawings for Tattoos," toured Williams College, the Joan Lehman Museum of Contemporary Art in Miami, and the Center for the Arts at Yerba Buena Gardens in San Francisco in 1996. An exhibit about all kinds of body alteration was shown at the Baylor Art Gallery in Austin, Texas, in 1995. It was titled "Trends in Mutilation."

47. Sanders, *Customizing the Body,* 18-20.

48. Arnold Rubin, "The Tattoo Renaissance," *Marks of Civilization* (Los Angeles: Museum of Cultural History, University of California, 1988) 234. In pages 233-60 Rubin discusses the tattoo artists who were seminal to the growth of tattooing as an artistic medium, changes in regulation, styles, and patronage.

49. Sanders, *Customizing the Body,* 28-32.

50. Sanders, *Customizing the Body,* 41.

51. Sanders, *Customizing the Body,* 42-43.

52. H. Drewal, 83.

53. Paul Bohannan, "Beauty and Scarification Amongst the Tiv," *Marks of Civilization* (Los Angeles: Museum of Cultural History, University of California, 1988), 82.

54. Sanders, *Customizing the Body,* 136.

55. Helen, interview by author, 23 September 1993, Austin, Texas. Helen is a 25-year-old graduate student who described her tattoo as a resolution of identity, career, and lifestyle decisions. She enjoyed the tattooing process and described it as "definitely sexual."

56. Steward, 57.

57. Steward, 65-68.

58. Z., interview by author, Austin, Texas, 1 April 1996. This interviewee was a tattoo artist who claimed that a few years prior to 1996 he tattooed several fraternity members a week. He claimed that now he tattoos very few fraternity members because they get pierced instead.

59. Quoted in Jan Seeger, "Do Unto Others," *Skin & Ink*, October 1993: 7.

60. Steward, 65.

61. The pain of the tattoo process varies with tattoo location, equipment used, and skill of the tattooist. Individuals also have differences in their ability to tolerate pain. Interestingly, tattooists note that women seem less disturbed by the pain than men (Sanders, *Customizing the Body*, 136-37).

62. James Myers, "Nonmainstream Body Modification: Genital Piercing, Branding, Burning, and Cutting," *Journal of Contemporary Ethnography* 21.3 (1992): 290-92.

63. Sanders, *Customizing the Body*, 43.

64. Myers, 292.

65. Quoted in Myers, 293.

66. Susannah, interview by author, Lancaster, Pennsylvania, 14 January 1994. Susannah got her first tattoo as a symbol of publicly announcing her homosexuality. See also interviews with Helen and Sarah.

67. Deborah Kapchan, "Moroccan Women's Body Signs," *Bodylore*, ed. Katherine Young (Knoxville: University of Tennessee Press, 1993), 14.

68. Kapchan, 7.

69. Kapchan, 16-19. Quote page 16.

70. R., interview by author, Austin, Texas, 22 March 1996.

71. Clinton Sanders, "Memorial Decoration: Women, Tattooing, and the Meanings of Body Alteration," *Michigan Quarterly Review* 30.1 (1991): 148-49. Also Daryl "Bear" Belmares, interview by author, Austin, Texas, 23 April 1994.

72. Sanders, "Memorial Decoration," 156.

73. Gutierrez, 429-43.

74. Wendy Chapkis, *Beauty Secrets: Women and the Politics of Appearance* (Boston: South End Press, 1986), 138.

75. Taylor, 99.

76. Myers, 295-96.

77. Daryl "Bear" Belmares, interview by author, 23 April 1994, Austin, Texas.

78. Sanders, *Customizing the Body*, 18-20.

79. Sanders, *Customizing the Body*, 2.

80. Peter M. Gollwitzer, "Striving for Specific Identities: The Social Reality of Self-Symbolizing," *Public Self and Private Self*, ed. Roy F. Baumeister (New York: Springer Verlag, 1986), 145-49.

81. Patrick Rogers and Rebecca Crandall, "Think of It As Therapy: Even the Suit and Tie Set Is into Piercing," *Newsweek* 13 May 1993: 65.

82. Belmares interview, 23 April 1994.

83. Myers, 268.

84. Rogers and Crandall, 65.

85. Steward, 56.

86. John Money, *Lovemaps: Clinical Concepts of Sexual/Erotic Health and Pathology, Paraphilia, and Gender Transposition in Childhood, Adolescence, and Maturity* (New York: Irvington, 1986), 81-82.

87. Steward, 53, 92.

88. Belmares interview, 1994.

89. Myers, 271.

90. Robert Love, "Not for Ears Only," *Rolling Stone* 22 Feb 1990: 19.

91. Rogers and Crandall, 65.

92. Rogers and Crandall, 65.

93. Austin, Texas, where Belmares operates his business, is approximately 25 percent Hispanic.

94. Belmares interview, 23 April 1994.

95. Daryl "Bear" Belmares, interview by author, Austin, Texas, 9 March 1996.

96. Belmares, 9 March 1996.

97. T., interview by author, Austin, Texas, 9 March 1996.

98. Vanessa Alvarez, interview by author, Austin, Texas, 17 April 1996.

99. Belmares, 9 March 1996.

100. Myers, 296.

101. Myers, 287-96. See also L.A. Kauffman, "Beauty Knows No Pain," *Elle* 8.11 (1993): 65-67.

102. Myers, 298.

103. Myers, 292.

104. Myers, 297.

105. Kauffman, 65-67.

106. Seeger, "Do Unto Others," 5-13.

107. See Jan Seeger, "Charting Ancient Waters with the Titans of Tribal," *Skin & Ink*, October 1993: 34-45, in which tattooists explain the cross-cultural origins of their designs.

108. Rogers and Crandall, 65.

109. Sanders, *Customizing the Body,* 34. Scholarly journals include *Tattootime,* founded in 1982, and *The Tattoo Historian.* Popular reading includes *Skin & Ink, Body Art,* and *Piercing Fans International Quarterly.*

110. Suzy Menkes, "Fetish or Fashion? Body Piercing Has Moved Into the Mainstream, But Why?" *New York Times* 21 November 1993: sec 9, 1, 9.

111. *New York Times* 11 June 1992: C3, col 3.

112. Tina Gaudoin, "The Devil Made Me Do It," *New York Times Magazine* 27 February 1994, Part 2: 22, 28, 32.

113. Thorstein Veblen, *The Theory of the Leisure Class: An Economic Study of Institutions* (New York: Macmillan, 1899), 167-87.

114. Belmares, 9 March 1996. I was surprised when I witnessed a piercing and the subsequent change in the client's mood. When I had tried to converse with him previous to the piercing he was dismissive, and slightly hostile to my ideas. After the piercing his mannerism had changed drastically as he volunteered personal information and glowed with good will. Although the biggest factor was probably relief of tension and anxiety about the piercing, I wondered if the act of piercing had chemically altered his mood.

115. Rieff, 13.

Chapter 5

1. Ginette Paris, *Pagan Grace: Dionysos, Hermes, and Goddess Memory in Daily Life*, trans. Joanna Mott (Dallas: Spring Publications, 1900), 47.

2. Paris, 58.

3. Lynda Nead, *The Female Nude: Art, Obscenity and Sexuality* (New York: Routledge, 1992), 66-67.

4. Maria T. Pramaggiore, "Resisting/Performing/Femininity: Words, Flesh and Feminism in Karen Finley's 'The Constant State of Desire,'" *Theatre Journal* 44.3 (1992): 269-90.

5. Sally Banes, *Greenwich Village 1963: Avant-Garde Performance and the Effervescent Body* (Durham: Duke University Press, 1993), 204-12. Among other specifics, Banes discusses the actor Robert Blossom, Ron Rice's play *The Queen of Sheba*, "Norman Mailer's essay "The White Negro," and the role of improvisation according to Amiri Baraka in *Blues People*.

6. Walt Whitman, *The Complete Poetry and Prose of Walt Whitman* (Garden City: Garden City Books, 1954), 79, 122, 123.

7. Robert Mapplethorpe, *Mapplethorpe* (New York: Random House, 1992).

8. Dick Hebdige, *Subculture: The Meaning of Style* (London: Methuen, 1979), 17.

9. Matthew Goulish, "Performance Art and the Tradition of Rebellion," *Chronicle of Higher Education* 22 September 1993: B3.

10. Victor Turner, "Variations on a Theme of Liminality," *Secular Ritual*, ed. S.F. Moore and B.G. Myerhoff (Amsterdam: Van Gorcum, Assen, 1977), 36-52. Quote page 45.

11. Ann Daly, *Done Into Dance: Isadora Duncan in America* (Bloomington: Indiana University Press, 1995), 120.

12. Thevoz, 23.

13. Martin Duberman, *Black Mountain: An Exploration in Community* (New York: W.W. Norton, 1993), 370-72.

14. RoseLee Goldberg, *Performance Art: From Futurism to the Present* (New York: Harry. N. Abrams, 1988), 129-30. Synopsis on page 152.

15. Linda Burnham, "Running Commentary," *High Performance* 11 (1988): 16.

16. Carolee Schneemann, *More Than Meat Joy: Complete Performance Works and Selected Writings* (New Paltz: Documentext and McPherson, 1979), 58.

17. Thevoz, 119. Pane's performance was titled "Psyche" and was performed at the Stadler Gallery in Paris, 1974.

18. Quoted in Thevoz, 119.

19. Podvall, 220.

20. Kathy O'Dell, "The Performance Artist as Masochistic Woman," *Arts Magazine* June/62 (1988): 96-98.

21. Rachel Rosenthal, "Stelarc, Performance and Masochism," *Obsolete Body/Suspensions/Stelarc*, ed. Stelarc and James D. Paffrath (Davis: J.P. Publications, 1984), 69-71.

22. Thevoz, 119.

23. Thevoz, 119.

24. Anonymously quoted in Suzanne Muchnic, "Wrestling the Dragon," *ARTnews* 89.10 (1990): 127.

25. Andrea Juno and V. Vale, eds., *Bob Flanagan: Supermasochist* (San Francisco: Re/Search Publications, 1993), 67-68.

26. Linda Montano in *Angry Women*, ed. A. Juno and V. Vale (San Francisco: Re/Search Publications, 1991), 52.

27. Patti Smith, "Gloria," *Horses* (Arista Records, 1975).

28. Favazza and Favazza, 199.

29. William Harris, "Demonized and Struggling with His Demons," *New York Times*, 23 October 1994: H31, H35.

30. Rudolph Arnheim, "Art as Therapy," *New Essays in the Psychology of Art* (Los Angeles: University of California Press, 1986), 257.

31. Michael Selzer, *Terrorist Chic: An Exploration of Violence in the Seventies* (New York: Hawthorn, 1979), 189.

32. Victor Bockris, *Uptight: The Story of the Velvet Underground* (New York: Quill, 1983), 75. This event occurred during the recording session for "European Son" in 1967.

33. Bockris, 42.

34. Bockris, 23.

35. Quoted in Tricia Henry, *Break All Rules! Punk Rock and the Making of a Style* (Ann Arbor: UMI Research Press, 1989), 18.

36. Clinton Heylin, *From the Velvets to the Voidoids: A Pre-Punk History for a Post-Punk World* (New York: Penguin, 1993), 41.

37. John Sinclair quoted in Heylin, 38.

38. Heylin, 39.

39. Thevoz, 126.

40. Thevoz, 126.

41. Henry, 97.

42. Henry, 2.

43. Lott, 81. The Bowery B'Hoy and his G'Hirl even became figures on the stage for a while in the characters of Mose and Liza, who portrayed Bowery working-class dress and mannerisms.

44. Lois W. Banner, *American Beauty* (New York: Alfred A. Knopf, 1983), 66-85.

45. Thevoz, 77.

46. Hebdige, 106-108, 151. Quote page 108.

47. Daniel Wojcik, *Punk and Neo-Tribal Body Art* (Jackson: University Press of Mississippi, 1985). Wojcik's book is a succinct account of punk's history, style, and repercussions including punk incorporation of body modification to shock viewers and function as a self-initiation into marginal status. It is beautifully illustrated with color photographs.

48. Selzer, xiv-xv.

49. Selzer, 145-50, 177-98, 191-93.

50. Selzer, 188, 191.

51. Selzer, 120-27.

52. Henry, 4-5. This behavior is recorded in the documentary *The Decline of Western Civilization*, a film about the punk scene in Los Angeles (Los Angeles: Speeris Films, Media Home Entertainment, distributed exclusively by Image Entertainment, 1985).

53. Hebdige, 63-64.

54. Hebdige, 115.

Conclusion

1. Podvall, 219.

2. Napier, 167-68.

3. Bruch, 6.

4. Bruch, 90.

5. Bruch, 20.

6. Bruch, 31.

7. Belmares, 9 March 1996.

8. Dienstfrey claims that 50 documented cases of stigmata exist (119).

9. Erving Goffman, *Stigma: Notes on the Management of a Spoiled Identity* (Englewood Cliffs: Prentice Hall, 1963), 1.

10. Awad Abdelgadir, interview by author, Austin, Texas, 19 April 1996.

11. Girard, 280-84.

12. Timo Araksinen, *Of Glamor, Sex, and De Sade* (Wakefield: Longwood Academic, 1991), 114.

Bibliography

Abenheimer, Karl M. "On Narcissism." *Narcissism, Nihilism, Simplicity and Self.* Edinburgh: Aberdeen University Press, 1991. 53-58.

Abdelgadir, Awad. Interview by author. Austin, Texas, 19 March 1996.

Agosin, Tomas. "Psychosis, Dreams and Mysticism in the Clinical Domain." Halligan and Shea 41-66.

Alvarez, Vanessa. Interview by author. Austin, Texas, 17 April 1996.

Amery, Francis. "Self-Sacrifice." *The Dedalus Book of Femme Fatales.* Ed. Bruce Stableford. Cambs, U.K.: Dedalus, 1992. 236-50.

Araksinen, Timo. *Of Glamor, Sex, and De Sade.* Wakefield: Longwood Academic, 1991.

Arnheim, Rudolph. "Art as Therapy." *New Essays in the Psychology of Art.* Los Angeles: University of California Press, 1986. 252-57.

Bakhtin, Mikhail. *Rabelais and His World.* Trans. by Helene Iswolsky. Bloomington: Indiana University Press, 1984.

Banner, Lois W. *American Beauty.* New York: Alfred A. Knopf, 1983.

Baumeister, Roy F. *Masochism and the Self.* Hillsdale: Lawrence Erlbaum Associates, 1989.

Bell, Rudolph M. *Holy Anorexia.* Chicago: University of Chicago Press, 1985.

Bellah, Robert et al. *Habits of the Heart: Individualism and Commitment in American Life.* Berkeley: University of California Press, 1985.

Belmares, Daryl "Bear." Interview by author. Austin, Texas, 23 April 1994.

——. Interview by author. Austin, Texas, 9 March 1996.

Benjamin, Jessica. "Master and Slave: The Fantasy of Erotic Domination." *Powers of Desire: The Politics of Sexuality.* Ed. Ann Snitow, Christine Stansell, and Sharon Thompson. New York: Monthly Review Press, 1983. 280-99.

Bentsen, Cheryl. *Maasai Days.* New York: Summit Books, 1989.

Bianchi, Robert S. "Tattoo in Ancient Egypt." Rubin 21-28.

Bilmes, Jacob, and Alan Howard. "Pain as Cultural Drama." *Anthropology and Humanism Quarterly* 5 (1980): 10-13.

Blume, E. Sue. "The Walking Wounded: Post-Incest Syndrome." *Siecus Report* 15.1 (1986): 5-7.

Bockris, Victor. *Up-tight: The Velvet Underground Story.* New York: Quill, 1983.

Bodanis, David. *The Body Book: A Fantastic Voyage to the World Within.* Boston: Little, Brown, 1984.

Bohannan, Paul. "Beautification and Scarification Amongst the Tiv." Rubin 77-82.

Bordo, Susan. "Anorexia Nervosa: Psychopathology as the Crystallization of Culture." *Feminism and Foucault: Reflections on Resistance.* Ed. Irene Diamand and Lee Quimby. Boston: Northeastern University Press, 1988. 87-111.

Brena, Steven. *Pain and Religion: A Psychological Study.* Springfield: Charles C. Thomas, 1972.

Bruch, Hilde. *The Golden Cage: The Enigma of Anorexia Nervosa.* Cambridge: Harvard University Press, 1978.

Brumberg, Joan Jacobs. *Fasting Girls: The Emergence of Anorexia as a Modern Disease.* Cambridge: Harvard University Press, 1988.

Burnham, Linda. "Running Commentary." *High Performance* 11 (1988): 16.

Carswell, John. *Coptic Tattoo Designs.* Beirut: American University of Beirut, 1958.

Cauwels, Janice M. *Bulimia: The Binge-Purge Compulsion.* Garden City: Doubleday, 1983.

Chapkis, Wendy. *Beauty Secrets: Women and the Politics of Appearance.* Boston: South End Press, 1986.

Chernin, Kim. *The Hungry Self: Women, Eating, and Identity.* New York: Times Books, 1985.

Chowanec, Gregory D., Allan M. Josephson, Charles Coleman, and Harry Davis. "Self-Harming Behavior in Incarcerated Male Delinquent Adolescents." *Journal of the American Academy of Child and Adolescent Psychiatry* 30.2 (1991): 202-07.

Cohen, Stanley, and Laurie Taylor. *Psychological Survival: The Experience of Long-Term Imprisonment.* New York: Pantheon, 1972.

Cordilia, Ann. *The Making of an Inmate: Prison As a Way of Life.* Cambridge: Schenkman, 1983.

"Correctional Architecture: The Symptoms of Neglect, The Signs of Hope." *Architectural Record* 150 (August 1971): 109-24.

Cosman, Madeleine Pelner. *Fabulous Feasts: Medieval Cookery and Ceremony.* New York: George Braziller, 1976.

Cushman, Philip. "Why the Self Is Empty: Toward a Historically Situated Psychology." *American Psychologist* 45.5 (1990): 599-611.

Daly, Ann. *Done Into Dance: Isadora Duncan in America.* Bloomington: Indiana University Press, 1995.

Dienstfrey, Harris. *Where the Mind Meets the Body.* New York: Harper-Collins, 1991.

Douglas, Mary. *Natural Symbols: Explorations in Cosmology.* New York: Vintage Books, 1970.

——. *Purity and Danger: An Analysis of Concepts of Pollution and Taboo.* London: Ark Paperbacks, 1966.

Drewal, Henry John. "Beauty and Being: Aesthetics and Ontology in Yoruba Body Art." *Marks of Civilization.* Ed. Arnold Rubin. Museum of Cultural History, University of California, 1988. 83-96.

——, and Margaret Thompson Drewal. *Gelede: Art and Female Power Among the Yoruba.* Bloomington: Indiana University Press, 1990.

Drewal, Margaret Thompson. "Portraiture and Construction of Reality in Yorubaland and Beyond." *African Arts* 23.2 (1990): 40-49.

Duberman, Martin. *Black Mountain: An Exploration in Community.* New York: W.W. Norton, 1993.

Ebin, Victoria. *The Body Decorated.* London: Blacker, Calmann Cooper, 1979.

Eisminger, Sterling. "The Curious Disposition of Body Parts, 1800-1850: Coincidence or Romantic Impulse?" *The Stiffest Corpse.* Ed. Andrei Codescu. San Francisco: City Lights Books, 1989. 222-24.

Eliade, Mircea. *Birth and Rebirth: The Religious Meanings of Initiation in Human Culture.* Trans. Willard R. Trask. New York: Harper, 1958.

——. *Rites and Symbols of Initiation: The Rites of Birth and Rebirth.* Trans. Willard R. Trask. New York: Harper, 1958.

Elias, Norbert. *The Civilizing Process: The History of Manners.* New York: Urizen Books, 1978.

Ellmann, Maud. *The Hunger Artists: Starving, Writing, and Imprisonment.* Cambridge: Harvard University Press, 1993.

Favazza, Armando R., and Barbara Favazza. *Bodies Under Siege: Self-Mutilation in Culture and Psychiatry.* Baltimore: Johns Hopkins Press, 1987.

——, and Karen Conterio. "Female Habitual Self-Mutilators." *Acta Psychiatria Scandinavia* 1129S (1988): 78-84.

——, and Karen Conterio. "The Plight of Chronic Self-Mutilators." *Community Mental Health Journal* 24.1 (1988): 22-30.

——, and Lori DeRosear. "Self-Mutilation and Eating Disorders." *Suicide and Life Threatening Behavior* 19.4 (1989): 352-62.

Feuerstein, Georg. *Yoga: The Technology of Ecstasy.* Los Angeles: Jeremy P. Tarcher, 1989.

Foucault, Michel. *Discipline and Punish: The Birth of the Prison* New York: Pantheon, 1977.

Frazer, James. *The New Golden Bough*. New York: New American Library, 1964.

Freud, Sigmund. "Animism, Magic and the Omnipotence of Thoughts." *Totem and Taboo*. New York: W.W. Norton, 1931. 94-124.

Garrard, Robert L. "Self-Mutilation." *Edgewood Medical Monographs* 1 (1950): 92-101.

Gaudoin, Tina. "The Devil Made Me Do It." *New York Times Magazine* Part 2, 27 February 1994: 22, 28, 32.

Girard, Rene. *Violence and the Sacred*. Trans. Patrick Gregory. Baltimore: Johns Hopkins University Press, 1977.

Goffman, Erving. *Asylums: Essays on the Social Situation of Mental Patients and Other Inmates*. Garden City: Anchor Books, 1961.

——. *Stigma: Notes on the Management of a Spoiled Identity*. Englewood Cliffs: Prentice Hall, 1963.

Goldberg, RoseLee. *Performance Art: From Futurism to the Present*. New York: Henry N. Abrams, 1988.

Goldman, Irving. *Ancient Polynesian Society*. Chicago: University of Chicago Press, 1970.

Gollwitzer, Peter M. "Striving for Specific Identities: The Social Reality of Self-Symbolizing." *Public Self and Private Self*. Ed. Roy F. Baumeister. New York: Springer Verlag, 1986. 145-49.

Goodsitt, A. "Self-Regulatory Disturbances in Eating Disorders." *International Journal of Eating Disorders* 2 (1983): 51-60.

Goulish, Matthew. "Performance Art and the Tradition of Rebellion." *Chronicle of Higher Education* 40.5 (22 September 1993): B3.

Gritton, Joy. "Labrets and Tattooing in Native Alaska." *Marks of Civilization*. Ed. Arnold Rubin. Los Angeles: Museum of Cultural History, University of California, 1988. 181-90.

Gutierrez, Nancy A. "Philomela Strikes Back: Adultery and Mutilation as Female Self-Assertion." *Women's Studies* 16 (1989): 429-43.

Haddon, Alfred C. *Magic and Fetishism*. London: Archibald Constable, Ltd. 1906.

Halligan, Frederica R., and John J. Shea, eds. *The Fires of Desire: Erotic Energies and the Spiritual Quest*. New York: Crossroad, 1992.

Hambly, W.D. *The History of Tattooing and Its Significance*. London: H.F.&G. Witherby, 1925.

Handy, E.S. Craighill, and Willowdean Chatterson Handy. *Samoan House Building, Cooking, and Tattooing*. Honolulu: Bernice P. Bishop Museum, 1924.

Harris, William. "Demonized and Struggling with His Demons." *New York Times* 23 October 1994, H31, H35.

Hawkins, R.E., and J.A. Popplestone. "The Tattoo as Exoskeletal Defense." *Perceptual and Motor Skills* 19.2 (1964): 500.

Hebdige, Dick. *Subculture: The Meaning of Style*. London: Methuen, 1979.

Helen. Interview by author. Austin, Texas, 23 September 1993.

Heller, Scott. "Philosopher Links Classical Texts and *Vogue* Models in a Study of Cultural Pressures on Women and Their Bodies." *Chronicle of Higher Education* 40.3 (8 September 1993): A10, A16.

Henderson, Joseph L. *Thresholds of Initiation*. Middletown: Wesleyan University Press, 1967.

Henry, Tricia. *Break All Rules! Punk Rock and the Making of a Style*. Ann Arbor: UMI Research Press, 1989.

Heylin, Clinton. *From the Velvets to the Voidoids: A Pre-Punk History for a Post-Punk World*. New York: Penguin, 1993.

Huxley, Aldous. *The Doors of Perception and Heaven and Hell*. 1955. New York: Harper, 1963.

James, William. *The Varieties of Religious Experience*. 1902. New York: New American Library, 1958.

Johnson, Elmer H., and Benjamin Britt. *Felon Self-Mutilation: Correlate of Stress in Prison*. Carbondale: Center for the Study of Crime, Delinquency, and Corrections, Southern Illinois University, 1969.

Juno, Andrea, and Vale, V., eds. *Angry Women*. San Francisco: Re/Search Publications, 1991.

——. *Bob Flanagan: Supermasochist*. San Francisco: Re/Search Publications, 1993.

Kafka, John S. "The Body as a Transitional Object: A Psychoanalytic Study of a Self-Mutilating Patient." *British Journal of Medical Psychology* 42.3 (1969): 207-12.

Kalweit, Holger, *Shamans, Healers, and Medicine Men*. Trans. Michael H. Kohn. Boston: Shambhala, 1992.

Kandel, R.F., and G.H. Pelto. "The Health Food Movement: Social Revitalization or Alternative Health Maintenance System?" Ed. N.W. Jerome et al. *Nutritional Anthropology: Contemporary Approaches to Diet and Culture*. Pleasantville: Redgrave, 1980. 328-63.

Kapchan, Deborah. "Moroccan Women's Body Signs." *Bodylore*. Ed. Katherine Young. Knoxville: University of Tennessee Press, 1993. 3-34.

Kaplan, Louise J. *Female Perversions: The Temptations of Madame Bovary*. New York: Doubleday, 1991.

Kauffman, L.A. "Beauty Knows No Pain." *Elle* 8.11 (1993): 65-67.

Kohut, Heinz. *The Restoration of the Self*. New York: International Universities Press, 1977.

Krueger, David W. *Body Self and Psychological Self: A Developmental and Clinical Integration of Disorders of the Self*. New York: Brunner/Mazel, 1989.

Lander, J., and H.M. Kohn. "A Note on Tattooing Among Selectees." *American Journal of Psychiatry* 100 (1943): 326-27.

Lasch, Christopher. *The Culture of Narcissism.* New York: W.W. Norton, 1979.

Lears, T.J. Jackson, *No Place of Grace: Antimodernism and the Transformation of American Culture 1880-1920* New York: Pantheon, 1981.

Leary, Timothy, Ralph Metzner, and Richard Alpert. *The Psychedelic Experience: A Manual Based on the Tibeten Book of the Dead.* New York: Carol Publishing Group, 1962.

Light, Douglas W. *Tattooing Practices of the Cree Indians.* Occasional Paper No. 6. Calgary: Glenbow-Alberta Institute.

Lott, Eric. *Love and Theft: Blackface Minstrelsy and the American Working Class.* New York: Oxford University Press, 1993.

Love, Robert. "Not for Ears Only." *Rolling Stone* 22 February 1990: 19.

M., Interview by author. Austin, Texas, 3 May 1996.

MacLeod, Sheila. *The Art of Starvation: A Story of Anorexia and Survival.* New York: Schocken, 1982.

MacSween, Morag. *Anorexic Bodies: A Feminist and Sociological Perspective on Anorexia Nervosa.* New York: Routledge, 1993.

Majno, Guido. *The Healing Hand: Man and the Wound in the Ancient World.* Cambridge: Harvard University Press, 1975.

Mapplethorpe, Robert. *Mapplethorpe.* New York: Random House, 1992.

Margolis, Dawn. "By Food Obsessed." *American Health* 15.3 (April 1996): 47.

Mascia-Lees, Frances E., and Patricia Sharpe, eds. *Tattoo, Torture, Mutilation, and Adornment: The Denaturalization of the Body in Culture and Text.* Albany: State University of New York Press, 1992.

Melville, Herman. *Moby Dick; or the Whale.* 1851. Berkeley: University of California Press, 1979.

Menkes, Suzy. "Fetish or Fashion? Body Piercing Has Moved to the Mainstream, But Why?" *New York Times* 21 November 1993, sec 9: 1, 9.

Mennell, Stephen. *All Manners of Food: Eating and Taste in England and France from the Middle Ages to the Present.* New York: Basil Blackwell, 1985.

Menninger, Karl. "A Psychoanalytic Study of the Significance of Self-Mutilation." *Psychoanalytic Quarterly* 4.3 (1935): 408-66.

Merleau-Ponty, Maurice. *Phenomenology of Perception.* Trans. Colin Smith. New York: Humanities Press, 1962.

Meyers, James. "Nonmainstream Body Modification: Genital Piercing, Branding, Burning, and Cutting." *Journal of Contemporary Ethnography* 21.3 (1992): 267-307.

Money, John. *The Destroying Angel: Sex, Fitness and Food in the Legacy of Degeneracy Theory, Graham Crackers, Kellogg's Corn Flakes and American Health History.* Buffalo: Prometheus, 1985.

——. *Lovemaps: Clinical Concepts of Sexual/Erotic Health and Pathology, Paraphilia, and Gender Transposition in Childhood, Adolescence, and Maturity.* New York: Irvington, 1986.

Moore, Robert L. "Decoding the Diamond Body: The Structure of the Deep Masculine and the Forms of the Libido." Halligan and Shea 111-25.

Morris, Desmond. "Body Adornment: Social Mutilations and Cosmetic Decorations." *Dimensions of Dress and Adornment.* Ed. Lois M. Gurel and Marianne S. Beeson. 3rd ed. Dubuque: Kendall/Hunt, 1975. 14-19.

Motoyama, Sono. "Hurts So Good: Whips, Chains, and Nipple Clamps —and the Nice Folks Next Door Who Use Them." *Baltimore City Paper* 17.3 (15 January 1992): 6-15.

Muchnic, Suzanne. "Wrestling the Dragon." *Artnews* 89.10 (1990): 125-29.

Mukai, Takao. "A Call for Our Language: Anorexia from Within." *Women's Studies International Forum* 12.6 (1989): 613-38.

Myers, James. "Nonmainstream Body Modification: Genital Piercing, Branding, Burning, and Cutting." *Journal of Contemporary Ethnography* 21.3 (1992): 267-307.

Napier, A. David. *Foreign Bodies: Performance, Art and Symbolic Anthropology.* Los Angeles: University of California Press, 1992.

Nead, Lynda. *The Female Nude: Art, Obscenity and Sexuality.* New York: Routledge, 1992.

O'Dell, Kathy. "The Performance Artist as Masochistic Woman." *Arts Magazine* 62 (1988): 96-98.

Orbach, Susie. *Hunger Strike: The Anorectic's Struggle as a Metaphor for Our Age.* New York: W.W. Norton, 1986.

Pandit, M.P., *Gems from the Tantras: Kularnava.* Madras, India: Ganesh, 1975.

Pao, Ping-Nie. "The Syndrome of Delicate Self-Cutting." *British Journal of Medical Psychology* 42 (1969): 195-206.

Paris, Ginette. *Pagan Grace: Dionysos, Hermes, and Goddess Memory in Daily Life.* Trans. Joanna Mott. Dallas: Spring Publications, 1990.

Parry, Albert. *Tattoo: Secrets of a Strange Act as Practised Among the Natives of the United States.* New York: Simon & Schuster, 1933.

——. "Tattoo Crisis." *Stories of Tramp Life.* Ed. E. Haldeman-Julius. Little Blue Book No. 1412. Girard: Haldeman-Julius Publications, 1929. 50-57.

——. "Tattooing Among Prostitutes and Perverts." *Psychoanalytic Quarterly* 3 (1934): 476-82.

Patterson, Orlando. *Slavery and Social Death: A Comparative Study.* Cambridge: Harvard University Press, 1982.

Pierce, Richard. "Tattooed Doll." *New York Times Magazine* 25 June 1995: 18.

Piersen, William D. *Black Legacy: America's Hidden Heritage.* Amherst: University of Massachusetts Press, 1993.

Podvall, Edward M. "Self-Mutilation Within a Hospital Setting: A Study of Identity and Social Compliance." *British Journal of Medical Psychology* 42.3 (1969): 213-21.

Porterfield, Amanda. *Female Piety in Puritan New England: The Emergence of Religious Humanism.* New York: Oxford University Press, 1992.

Post, R.S. "The Relation of Tattoos to Personality Disorder." *Journal of Criminal Law, Criminology, & Police Science* 59.4 (1968): 516-24.

Pramaggiore, Maria T. "Resisting/Performing/Femininity: Words, Flesh and Feminism in Karen Finley's 'The Constant State of Desire.'" *Theatre Journal* 44.3 (1992): 269-90.

Previte, Joseph. *Human Physiology.* New York: McGraw Hill, 1983.

R. Interview by author, Austin, Texas, 22 March 1996.

Raboteau, Albert J. *Slave Religion: The "Invisible" Institution in the Antebellum South.* New York: Oxford University Press, 1978.

Rapoport, Judith L. *The Boy Who Couldn't Stop Washing: The Experience and Treatment of Obsessive-Compulsive Disorder.* New York: New American Library, 1989.

Rieff, Philip. *The Triumph of the Therapeutic: Uses of Faith after Freud.* 1966. Chicago: University of Chicago Press, 1987.

Roberts, Allen F. "Tabwa Masks: An Old Trick of the Human Race." *African Arts* 23.2 (1990): 36-47.

Rodin, Judith. *Body Traps: Breaking the Binds That Keep You from Feeling Good About Your Body.* New York: William Morrow, 1992.

Rogers, Patrick, and Rebecca Crandall. "Think of It As Therapy: Even the Suit and Tie Set Is Into Piercing." *Newsweek* 13 May (1993): 65.

Rosenthal, Rachel. "Stelarc, Performance and Masochism." Ed. Stelarc and James D. Paffrath. *Obsolete Body/Suspensions/Stelarc.* Davis: J.P. Publications, 1984.

Ross, Robert Robertson, and Hugh Bryan McKay. *Self-Mutilation.* Lexington: Lexington Books, 1979.

Rubin, Arnold, ed. *Marks of Civilization: Artistic Transformations of the Human Body.* Los Angeles: Museum of Cultural History, University of California, 1988.

——. "The Tattoo Renaissance." *Marks of Civilization.* Museum of Cultural History, University of California, 1988. 233-60.

Rudofsky, Bernard. *The Unfashionable Human Body*. Garden City: Anchor Press, 1974.

Sagan, Eli. *Cannabalism: Human Aggression and Cultural Form*. New York: Harper, 1974.

Saitoti, Tepilit Ole. *The Worlds of A Maasai Warrior: An Autobiography*. New York: Random House, 1986.

Sanders, Clinton. *Customizing the Body: The Art and Culture of Tattooing*. Philadelphia: Temple University Press, 1989.

——. "Memorial Decoration: Women, Tattooing, and the Meanings of Body Alteration." *Michigan Quarterly Review* 30.1 (1991): 146-57.

Sarah. Personal interview. Austin, Texas, 9 March 1996.

Scarry, Elaine. *The Body in Pain: The Making and Unmaking of the World*. New York: Oxford University Press, 1985.

Schneemann, Carolee. *More Than Meat Joy: Complete Performance Works and Selected Writings*. New Paltz: Documentext & McPherson, 1979.

Schwartz, Hillel. *Never Satisfied: A Cultural History of Diets, Fantasies, and Fat*. New York: Free Press, 1986.

Seeger, Jan. "Charting Ancient Waters with the Titans of Tribal." *Skin & Ink* October 1993: 34-45.

——. "Do Unto Others." *Skin & Ink* October 1993: 4-13.

Selzer, Michael. *Terrorist Chic: An Exploration of Violence in the Seventies*. New York: Hawthorn, 1979.

Shaw, Miranda. *Passionate Enlightenment: Women in Tantric Buddhism*. Princeton: Princeton University Press, 1994.

Shea, Steven J., and Mary Craig Shea, "Self-Mutilatory Behavior in a Correctional Setting." *Corrective and Social Psychiatry and Journal of Behavior Technology Methods and Therapy* 37.4 (1991): 64-67.

Sinclair, A.T. "Tattooing—Oriental and Gypsy." *American Anthropologist* 10.3 (1908): 361-86.

Smith, Patti. "Gloria." *Horses*. Arista Records, 1975.

Sours, John A. *Starving to Death in a Sea of Objects: The Anorexia Syndrome*. New York: Jason Aronson, 1980.

Spheeris Films. "The Decline of Western Civilization." Media Home Entertainment distributed exclusively by Image Entertainment, 1985.

Spindler, Konrad. *The Man in the Ice: The Discovery of a 5,000 Year-Old Body Reveals the Secrets of the Stone Age*. New York: Harmony Books, 1994.

Steele, Valerie. *Fetish: Fashion, Sex, and Power*. New York: Oxford University Press, 1996.

Steward, Samuel M. *Bad Boys and Tough Tattoos: A Social History of the Tattoo with Gangs, Sailors, and Street-Corner Punks, 1950-1965*. New York: Harrington Park Press, 1990.

Stoller, Robert J. *Pain and Passion: A Psychologist Explores the World of S&M*. New York: Plenum Press, 1991.

Sugarman, A., and C. Karash. "The Body as Transitional Object in Bulimia." *International Journal of Eating Disorders* 1 (1982): 57-67.

Susannah. Interview by author. Lancaster, Pennsylvania, 14 January 1994.

T. Interview by author. Austin, Texas, 9 March 1996.

Taylor, A.J.W. "Tattooing among Male and Female Offenders of Different Ages in Different Types of Institutions." *Genetic Psychological Monographs* 81.1 (1970): 81-119.

Thevoz, Michel. *The Painted Body: Illusions of Reality*. New York: Rizzoli, 1984.

Thoreau, Henry David. *Walden and Civil Disobedience*. 1854. New York: Penguin, 1983.

Tiemersma, Douwe. *Body Schema and Body Image: An Interdisciplinary and Philosophical Study*. Amsterdam: Swets & Zeitlinger, 1989.

Toch, Hans. *Living in Prison: The Ecology of Survival*. New York: Free Press, 1977.

——. *Men in Crisis: Human Breakdowns in Prison*. Chicago: Aldine, 1975.

Turner, Victor. *The Ritual Process: Structure and Anti-Structure*. Chicago: Aldine, 1969.

——. "Variations on a Theme of Liminality." *Secular Ritual*. Ed. S.F. Moore and B.G. Myerhoff. Amsterdam: Van Gorcum, Assen, 1977. 36-52.

U.S. Bureau of Prisons. *Recent Prison Construction 1950-1960*. U.S. Bureau of Prisons, 1960.

Van Gennep, Arnold. *The Rites of Passage*. Trans. by Monika B. Vizedon and Gabrielle L. Caffee. Chicago: University of Chicago Press, 1960.

Veblen, Thorstein. *The Theory of the Leisure Class: An Economic Study of Institutions*. New York: Macmillan, 1899.

Vogel, Susan. "Baule Scarification: The Mark of Civilization." *Marks of Civilization*. Ed. Arnold Rubin. Los Angeles: Museum of Cultural History, University of California, 1988. 97-105.

Walker, Sheila S. *Ceremonial Spirit Possession in Africa and Afro-America: Forms, Meanings and Functional Significance for Individuals and Social Groups*. Leiden, Netherlands: E.J. Brill, 1972.

Weigle, Marta. *Brothers of Light: Brothers of Blood: The Penitents of the Southwest*. Albuquerque: University of New Mexico Press, 1976.

Weil, Andrew. *The Marriage of the Sun and the Moon: A Quest for Unity in Consciousness*. Boston: Houghton Mifflin, 1980.

Whitman, Walt. *The Complete Poetry and Prose of Walt Whitman*. 1948. Garden City: Garden City Books, 1954.

Wojcik, Daniel. *Punk and Neo-Tribal Body Art*. Jackson: University Press of Mississippi, 1985.

Woodman, Marion. *Addiction to Perfection: The Still Unravished Bride*. Toronto: Inner City Books, 1982.

Woolson, Abba Goold. *Woman in American Society*. Boston: Roberts Brothers, 1873.

Yates, Alayne. "Current Perspectives on the Eating Disorders. I. History, Psychological, and Biological Aspects." *Journal of the American Academy of Child and Adolescent Psychiatry* 28.6 (1989): 813-28.

Z. Interview by author. Austin, Texas, 1 April 1996.

Index